Into the Dimensions

Into the Dimensions

My Paranormal and
Extraterrestrial Experiences
Volume One

Written by
Carlo S. Carnevalini

***

Edited by
Peter Anthony Flynn

Published at Amazon by
Peter Anthony Flynn

Illustrations by
Osman Ariel Salgado Espinoza

Printed by Amazon

ISBN 9781796432831

To my mother

Justina Pasquier

who not only gave me the gift of life,
but also for genetically transferring
the gift of seeing past where
the human eye cannot see!

Table of Contents

Foreword

I have known Carlo since 2012. As a researcher and science fiction writer, I'm always very interested in interviewing experiencers and abductees to gain insights and knowledge. At MUFON LA, I met Carlo who became one of the first experiencers to let me into his private world of paranormal and extraterrestrial events. This is because we developed a profound, mutual trust right from the start. At the same time, I was very fascinated by his stories whose basic elements regarding UFOs, ETs and a variety of paranormal activity showed me new dimensions in this world as well as the Universe.

The one thing in common with most experiencers I have since observed is that they often have a lineage of relatives, past and present, who have had similar experiencers. This is because the paranormal and extraterrestrial beings tend to follow the energy signatures of families down through the generations. I have also observed that at some point an ancestor's DNA was often directly linked to some extraterrestrial race. Once an experiencer has this enhancement, they also can perceive paranormal activity on Earth.

I've read reports that we have up to 97% ET DNA while utilizing only 3% of our so-called human DNA. This is an alarming discovery which Earth scientists are just beginning to recognize as a fact. As for the paranormal beings like ghosts or those beings living in hidden dimensions that Carlo has stepped into, they are all related in terms of the dimensions. This means that they all exist in a higher frequency which only a few humans are gifted enough to view. Thus, you do have your uncanny psychics and clairvoyants who can see into the near future, as is the case with Carlo.

I recognize Carlo's stories as the truth. He is not motivated to lie. His life has been so affected since his first ET experience as a little boy of 5 that he has lived a virtual nightmare of 100s of experiences extending into his middle years. I invite you to be an observer by reading these heartfelt and soulful stories which reveal a hidden and mysterious world beyond our normal reality.

Peter Anthony Flynn

<u>Acknowledgments</u>

I wish to express my sincere gratitude to my friend Peter Anthony Flynn, owner of RollPix Escripts, for coming to my rescue, and for his good heart. Peter helped me to finally share all these true but strange stories with the world out there.

I thank my family for believing in me and for all their support to help me in carrying out this project. I would also like to thank each member of my mom's side of the family, the Pasquiers, who have confirmed that paranormal events are true in their lives and in the same area where I had many of my experiences. I'm grateful for them, especially for inspiring me to complete my next book.

Lastly, I would like to give acknowledgment to several, benevolent, humanoid ETs with whom I interacted in my off world experiences. They inspired me to bring back messages of truth to Earth. I have fondly named them Elizabeth, Suzanne, Hannah and Mrs. Farnsworth.

Introduction

The title of my book was inspired by the way I always felt during my whole life. Every time I got to survive any paranormal activity, my life wasn't any easier. It followed me everywhere like a curse. It was my perverse gift from fate: the curse of the gifted. I felt used, persecuted, and condemned by these spellbinding experiences. I always dreamed of being a simple guy with a straightforward life. Instead of that, what I was left with was a miserable journey. I felt doomed, because I couldn't figure out how to stop what life had in store for me.

At the same time, I firmly confess that I'm thankful and wouldn't change my experiences for anything more or anything less than what I have already lived regardless of my complaints. I'd give all I have to live my whole life all over again and have the same experiences. I also firmly believe that many conspiracy theories are nothing but certain truths in this mad and ridiculous world. Humanity lives a lie—a fairytale—and we all are sleeping inside a crystal ball. The world as we know it is being manipulated by invisible evil forces. They control humanity (the sheep, the blind, the masses). I got to see it with my own eyes—a made-up reality prepared to make us believe that we're safe when we're not. I realized that the world is nothing but a big circus full of clowns dressed in suits, and they get to make our choices. We just go along believing those choices are ours when they're not. This is to keep us from a need to look over the rainbow, so to speak, when we really need to keep our eyes open like hawks.

I've made my peace by writing these stories to depict "the hidden" and the different worlds out there. They're right here in front of us, but we can't see them because only the gifted like me can do so. These worlds have always existed, and they're right under our noses. My stories were inspired by my own true experiences, both paranormal and extraterrestrial. My dream now is that those who wake up are aware once and for all and become kinder towards their fellow human beings of all races.

Finally, I have used pseudonyms for the real persons in my non-fiction stories in order to protect their true identity.

Carlo S. Carnevalini

Into the Dimensions

1.

The UFO Invasion

"I saw countless alien ships orbiting our world."

In 1979 I escaped the civil war in Nicaragua and moved to the USA temporarily. My older brothers were already living in California at a cousin's home, but when I arrived, we were too crowded for comfort, and so they decided to move away on their own. My older brother Erick was 19 at the time. He found a job in a clothing factory and moved into his own place. He asked me if I wanted to live with him so we wouldn't have to be a burden to our kind-hearted relatives. We had escaped the genocide of a civil war and were very thankful God had spared our lives. It was kind of embarrassing being at someone's home without contributing financially. I was happy to move away with my brother immediately.

Erick's apartment was a small, furnished studio in the Los Angeles area near Hollywood, located right by Vermont Avenue and 3rd Street. I was happy regardless of the building looking kind of old and rundown although the interior looked fairly clean. What I loved the most was the fact that we were close to everything we needed, including a great, family-run, inexpensive food-to-go place. The special of the day served everyday was white rice, black beans, deep fried sweet plantains, and Milanese steak. How to forget the jalapeño sauce? It was such a great delicious Cuban food— the best in town back then. The old building on Vermont Avenue still stands there to this day. What I'd never see again was that delicious, Cuban food-to-go place; what a bummer. Our apartment number was 303 on the third floor across from the elevator. We despised the unbearable noise all day from the elevator, but eventually like magic, one day, a few weeks later, it didn't bother us anymore, thank God.

The landlord in that building was a nice guy named Isaac. We became friends very quickly and frequented each other's place on a daily basis. Isaac was around 28 years old and had a red beard and a slim build, not too tall yet taller than me. I was around sixteen at the time, but I was very eager to befriend anyone. I felt lonely; I knew no one in such a huge city. I also learned that Isaac was a struggling writer and that he was making financial ends meet for years with his talent. He told me that he was positive that one day Hollywood was going to give him his big break and that he would stop bouncing around. Personally, I thought that he was kidding with me because in my head, and coming from a little country like mine, that was a big joke. Later, I realized that he was dead serious and that was when I stopped laughing. After all of that, we became really close. Isaac was also a freelance photographer and a handyman. He managed that building to secure his rent, and I started to admire his ingenuity.

Isaac told me that he also wrote scripts for a few TV shows that I'd rather not mention. I was a newcomer in the USA and didn't know much about that stuff, but I did see his name on the credits at the end of some popular series. My new friend would show me photo slides of awesome Asian cities, beautiful landscapes, and all kinds of people of different races. He projected his pictures on his living room wall with a Kodak projector for slides, which he kept in his living room closet. I was impressed to see that Isaac had a variety of pretty girls traveling and hiking with him into amazing and incredible places. He showed me astonishing close ups of flying insects, humming birds feeding on the nectar of flowers, rock formations in the Grand Canyon in Colorado, and the wonderful Yuma desert dunes along the flanks of the Gila Mountains in Arizona. Isaac was cool like that. After the free nightly show, I would go back to my brother's studio and dream about the stories Isaac shared with me. I thought to myself that one day I would also travel the world and materialize Isaac's stories with my own adventures.

For months, Isaac also read to me a lot of his writing material to hear my opinion. I was limited with my English but could tell if I liked what I heard or not. He also loaned me some of his books to embrace his American culture. He became some sort of a mentor to me, helped me correct my limited English at the time, and taught me how to pronounce a few difficult words that sounded weird when I tried to express myself on my own.

Isaac was good therapy for me. Soon enough, he knew that I was a young man who had just left a country filled with thousands of horror stories and plenty of traumatic experiences no one would wish on their worst enemy. I trusted Isaac enough to confess my miserable tragedy. I told him about all of the people I knew who had been killed and that I was badly affected with inner fears. I never had the courage to tell Isaac that I cried myself to sleep almost every night. I didn't understand or even care why we had a war; all I wanted was to lead a normal life again in my own country. I dreamed of freedom and liberty; I wanted to be respected and appreciated as a human being, the same way people felt in the USA.

Back in my country, I was used to having a fun life with my friends at any given time as any normal teenager before tragedy struck and the civil war killed my dreams and my emotional stability. In California I found that peace and safety I needed to feel alive and hopeful again. My brother Erick worked all the time. My responsibility was to go to school and return home to cook an easy meal for the both of us (usually boiled potatoes or onion soup). I sat around all day until my brother showed up tired and sleepy. We barely exchanged a few words because he had to get up early every day to go back to work. It was a factory where he joked around with a funny smile and told me that they worked him to death like a slave to earn his money. We managed to pay for our bills, food and rent. I tried to help my brother with what I could do at the time by at least keeping the place clean and other little activities. Meanwhile, I read books that Isaac loaned me to catch up with the English language stories, very easy to understand from amazing authors like Mark Twain and Herman Melville. I'd read them while I did our laundry.

I usually met with Isaac at lunch time to get a free TV meal so I didn't have to cook the same horrible mashed potatoes or onion soup which I left on top of the stove for Erick to eat. He never complained about it. Isaac helped me to learn English very fast and lose my Latino accent in no time.

One day out of the blue, I went to the basement to do my laundry again. It was a strange day. I experienced a weird rush that went from my feet to the hairs on my head. This was something very unusual for what I called my paranormal experiences because they usually happened to me mostly at night when I was about to fall asleep or in the middle of my dreams.

The result of these rushes affected my immediate perception. The reality that I was living at the moment would be disturbed to such a degree that I wouldn't know which of my realities would get me in trouble. Everything around me turned to slow motion. When these things happened to me in the past, even if I were alert, my mind got dazed and lost. As I was experiencing this strange phenomenon, Isaac showed up friendly as usual, and I recall that he was excited to talk to me about something that I couldn't make any sense of at the moment. In my mind, I was far away in la-la-land hearing loud sounds that perturbed my concentration. In other words, I was not being me; I was in the middle of chaos in a battle zone. I couldn't understand a single word Isaac said to me. I know I was annoyed, couldn't breathe, and panic was taking over. What I felt he saw was that I was acting weird and behaving too bizarrely to be understood. The pressure was building by the minute. I knew the best thing for Isaac to do was to leave me alone and avoid me completely. Since he wasn't doing that, I ran away from him. I knew something had happened, but I couldn't guess what to be honest, so I imagined by sleeping it off, I would get better and then explain my actions to him later on.

So, once inside my own place, I lay down on my bed and rested for a while. I remembered it was between one and two in the afternoon. Suddenly, I heard the sounds of celestial harps strangely playing in my head with subtle effects on me. The music went through me with harmony, and I became extremely relaxed. When, unexpectedly, an electrifying sound wave pierced my brain, I felt my body tremble from head to toe. It was unbearable. I could hardly breathe or move. My eyes rolled to the back of my head as if an unseen force possessed me. It was more like having an epileptic fit.

At that point, I was terrified by strange noises that freaked the hell out of me. The weirdness terrorized me. Then, I heard a loud **"*bang*."** It came out of nowhere. I was catapulted through the air and whizzed by a great speed when a colorful and bright disturbance entered my reality. A vortex opened up right above me in the ceiling like a tornado in slow motion. Everything else around melted away having another realm take over mine. It truly challenged all rules of logical reasoning and physics. It happened so fast and rapidly, I had no time to react, nor had any control over my surroundings. I knew that power had supernatural origins. Nothing in my world could do such a thing unless it was a science fiction movie effect, yet what happened to me that day was very tangible and real.

I felt every particle of my physical body trembling when I passed through these strange pockets of air and electrified lighting. This amazing and extraordinary experience was one of a series of events that started happening to me for years after this bizarre encounter. I was only sixteen back then. I was carried away as if I had wings; it was like nothing I can describe with my knowledge. A strange force held me in place, and I felt I had a sense of direction leading my way. I'd never had that kind of experience so vividly despite my trance state at the moment.

Next thing I knew was that I was inside what seemed to be a humongous warehouse. Years later, I figured out that the place had to be a SPACECRAFT, perhaps stationed outside Earth's atmosphere. The first thing I recall seeing in there was the most amazing view in multiple dimensions. I wondered why there were such huge walls and ceilings so high up that I felt like a tiny ant standing in there. I remember looking up and down through an opening and into a majestic and marvelous, intensely black, firmament full of what looked like beautiful diamonds in a fabric of heavens and twinkling stars that laid there in midair before my eyes. My amazement was such that my mind couldn't conceive such greatness.

My first thought was, "Who built this?"

Those words echoed in my head as if something inside told me that I was heard by "other beings" who were listening to my most inner thoughts of that great event. My logic told me that what I saw was an extraterrestrial spaceship of sorts. I wouldn't say that it was an alien ship because my head rushed with thousands of possibilities and immediate responses, but I knew deep in my heart that nothing made sense in my condition.

Although I had little knowledge about these things, now I am sure that what I saw then was a "mothership" outside our earthly atmosphere. I couldn't see that with my eyes but that is the most logical explanation in my mind, and I would agree after so many years because of what happened next. Clearly and tangibly, I recall that I saw myself wearing a white robe, which caressed my skin like a silk cover placed over my body. I was barefooted and totally naked under the robe. The place was magical to me. I felt my bare feet comfortable on the texture of the floors, which felt like the finest marble I had ever walked on. It made me not feel afraid.

The place was like a docking station of sorts, like a high place above the Earth with a magnificent view. My curiosity naturally began to scan the place and the small details around this huge space building modeled to store who knows what. I had never seen anything like it before on Earth, but I knew deep in my mind that it had to be a spacecraft because, looking up or down the huge window overlooking the vastness of outer space, there was nothing holding this enormous structure that I was in. There was no sense of physical movement in any direction either, yet I could see movement in space peeking out the window. Amazingly, that huge structure was moving in space but felt like it was on solid ground.

I don't remember seeing people, other beings, or doors as we know them on Earth, but I do remember I felt the presence of other intelligence besides me in that place. I felt the texture of metal that covered the craft, not made of any metal I had ever seen because it felt so soft to the touch as if it were moldable any which way, yet totally solid and firm. I didn't know what to think of it. The truth is that I didn't think; I only reacted to the surroundings, details, shapes, or forms that made my mind wonder with such amazement, or I reacted to what my eyes kept encountering at every step.

The temperature inside that place was totally under control, comfortable, and made me feel that I was in my own Earthly environment. I walked naturally and did not float as the astronauts floated in space. My body also didn't feel as if I weighed the 120 pounds I weighed back then, but as if it were made of a synthetic material, yet feelings and thoughts were totally untouched.

The dimensions of that place were of great proportions, but I wasn't lucky enough to see any form of flying control, switches or buttons to make sense of a craft hovering or flying along in the middle of the firmament.

Then, a voice inside my head, or perhaps in the air, a soundless voice but with authority, commanded me, "Don't look at me."

I felt a grab on my right shoulder. I was in a position where I couldn't avoid it. I followed whatever I was told without hesitation. Out of the corner of my eye, I felt a GIANT BEING next to me, at least two, even three times taller than me, yet, the stature had nothing to do with the way

I felt at that very instant. I felt welcomed; I knew in my heart I had the need to trust that being, and I did. I knew I was in a place where no harm would come to me.

As incredible as it sounds, its presence made me feel safe. The warmth that he radiated had the same effect as when my dad was around assuring me that everything was going to be all right and, in my heart and mind, I would blindly believe it. I found myself looking down at the floor because, for some reason under this sort of trance, I needed to concentrate on a specific point and that was usually to look downward to my feet. The illuminated floors turned glassy and transparent, and I had the impression of floating but with a firm step.

Then, the same voice said to me, "Look over there."

I turned my face back towards the subject. I saw Earth with its majestic white and blue colors. I was at a distance where I couldn't see anything but the oceans and the shape of the Earth plastered with clouds, like a painting about to take shape. I couldn't see anything else besides what I described. The Earth was illuminated like a light bulb and all around there was darkness and nothing else but blinking stars very far, so far away that I saw them the same size as they're seen from the ground.

The magnificent structure seemed to move forward towards the Earth, but still, I couldn't feel any movement like the pulling of my physical body. Next, I had many revelations. I can't explain them with words exactly how the lessons worked. It was a total mystery to me. I will need a few life times to begin to have an opinion about that. All I know is that it was in a different level of understanding not exactly with the human mind because it is limited, very fragile and defective as well. I had this curiosity to look around and see what no one with human eyes had ever seen; I knew I was a lucky guy, scared to death but lucky. Scared to death because I was chosen to experience what only a handful of humans could experience in a lifetime, namely an incredible adventure where someone out there came from a distance of millions of light years to my own world, noticed me, and picked me up to express what is hidden to humanity and to the world.

"Who was I?" I asked myself to be noticed by someone who considered me this important when I thought of myself as nothing more than a little peasant from Nicaragua, a nobody, someone who's not even special in any way. "Why was I chosen when I had nothing to offer?"

However, these questions were answered.

As the huge ship got closer to Earth, the Giant Being pointed with his large, five-fingered hand, and said, "Look."

He then pointed in all directions in and around the world as we know it.

My heart started beating fast, and again I felt a lot of fear. I saw countless alien ships orbiting our world just like mad African bees populating their hive, as if "they" owned our world.

The Giant Being was a benevolent being! He was letting me in on the secret hidden from humanity! He wanted me to know that we are living our lives as we see fit but behind the curtain something more was taking place! Our true reality! We were being invaded by an infestation of evil beings that worked hand in hand with the world leaders and that we were no more important to them than farm or jungle animals but that we were necessary to serve their plans!

Why was he sharing this with me you may ask yourself? Because our souls are infinite, and that was not the end of the story for us. He wanted to let me know that there was hope, and that no matter what, his kind had everything under control! I knew that I wasn't as important as some people may think just for the reason that they chose to tell me certain truth, but because I was a direct descendant of other beings before me of whom the promises were given. All their descendants were going to be the bearer of this truth, and that

I should write about it! The world would listen, and I shouldn't worry about the enemies of my ancestral family.

I was told by this Giant Being that although the dark seems to be winning the battle all the time or most of the time, loves prevails, the truth always wins and that we need to be conscious of how we carry our souls, our lives, and what makes us who we truly are. He told me that our bodies are a jail constructed by the evilest beings, the Reptilians. Originally, we were spiritually made in the image of the highest being (The Source), and our bodies were able to transcend time, distance and be immortal. But when the Reptilians got involved, they saw the opportunity to invade us by building a jail to trap us. This is their plan; it isn't The Source's plan that we die so young, that we become ill, or that we are limited.

The Reptilians are a race that has acquired all knowledge as we know it, but only in the physical sense. They, of course, managed to control some of the spiritual aspects of our lives as well. They are an older race and have outsmarted human beings because our bodies are designed to die in 100 years, more or less. By contrast, Reptilians can live for hundreds of years in one lifetime. They also can recreate their bodies. They have special abilities that make them supermen and women. They can store more knowledge in their physical bodies than we can because we are limited. They made us mortals because they mixed our DNA to last only for so long. Plus, they fabricated what makes us happy: drugs, alcohol, fake foods, and chemicals that feed us to only die along the way. They learned what made us tick; in our world it is called temptations. All these temptations are a game where humans become losers through sex, money, fame, success, fast food, fake juices, sodas, and insignificant things like French Fries or sweets.

Then our bodies fall apart with diseases not only physically but spiritually. Pride divides us and power corrupts our lives. Imposing a master mind over others also is a sign of power and makes humans sick in their souls. This Giant Being told me that breaking these schemes and being merciful, good and loving only makes us better humans. Our souls are trapped in these bodies, but that won't stop our positive vibes from saving our world even if darkness seems to win all the time. Such in not the case. We are only visualizing what we see with our eyes. What we need to invest in spiritually is for the moment when we have to depart this world.

Everything we do is accounted for, and that's what can makes us great and make the world go around. I know that I am not better than anyone; I know I can be miserable in my observations sometimes, also very human, and make lots of mistakes, but that doesn't make me a bad human. What makes us bad humans is seeing with our eyes the wrong of others and accepting it as normal, moral and true, or identifying with evil as if it were good when we know exactly that it is not.

So again, "Why do they tell me these things?" I asked myself over and over.

I am not hand-picked to be told. Rather, I am a part of a generation the promises were given to. There are thousands like me, and the rest of humanity just goes with the flow. Now, I'm writing about it. I was always told to write about it, but I was fearful of being attacked and of others thinking that I was a nutcase. But now I am standing up and risking it all.

This Giant Being is among other benevolent beings who are like an organization on Earth that can pinpoint the issues of our culture, society and politics, but they are not allowed to interfere, as I understand it, from what he expressed through telepathy. As a human race, we decide what we want by the way we react, choose, prefer, feel and vote in our hearts about how we want to be handled by our governments, politicians, police force, army, etc. These benevolent beings are respectful of our decisions. We are in this turmoil and hell hole because "we," the majority, chose it that way. There's always a minority that suffers. In order to see a significant change, we have to have more allies, and that's going to be very difficult because humanity is hypnotized into the luxuries of power, self- indulgence and vainglory in a money-based world. We just don't care as a whole human race and only think inside the box. We forgot that we are the human race. We strongly believe what our governments and politicians say to us. So as a privileged race or nation, we look the other way and care less about what's going on in other countries. The day we decide that we are one race, the human race, we'll see changes. Meanwhile, we are doomed and won't be able to free ourselves of this imminent death.

***

The experience was over as quickly as it had begun. I re-appeared on the rooftop of my building. There were some chairs and chase lounges up there that tenants would use sometimes to observe the night sky or talk or just to smoke.

I remember I was just looking down to Earth, and tears were running down my face non-stop. I couldn't help it. The Giant Being was soothing my spiritual and physical inner pain with his telepathic connection, and then I was in another place acting distraught, weird and confused in my own reality. It seemed that I passed from one surreal scene into the next with the power of thought.

I remember I was so fearful for hours until I went back to the apartment and dropped into bed. I didn't get up until my brother knocked on the door. We only had one key to the apartment in those days since Erick had lost his key, so I had to be there when he returned from work. He was really pissed because he said he'd been knocking for some time. I remember I was very, very tired. Usually, when I let him in we always shared his days, new experiences and had dinner

14

together but, on that evening, we just went straight to sleep without any further explanation!

***

A few days later after this experience, I still kept it to myself. I never shared my story with anyone. I was afraid people would mock me. So, I tried to bottle it all up, but I had the need to at least communicate something to someone. There was this feeling about needing to share my story, but I didn't know how to. Everything seemed incredible, and I had a hard time trying to understand it myself.

I know I couldn't share this experience with my brother Erick. He never believed me anyway and always belittled me for it.

The only person who came to mind was Isaac, yet I was so embarrassed for what happened in the basement. Perhaps he would not recall or be concerned about my weirdness because I was a young fellow, but I was wrong. I armed myself with courage and went straight up to see him in his apartment. I was going to explain myself in detail to gain his trust back.

So, I took the elevator and went to his apartment down on the first floor. I rang the bell twice.

"Come in!" said a raspy voice, that of an older man.

I pushed the door in and saw a chubby, hairy man with an old tank undershirt exposing most of his body fat. He seemed busy, raised an eyebrow, and with a gesture he kind of greeted me. I looked around and Isaac's stuff wasn't there any longer.

"Hi!" I said.

"Can I help you?" he replied barely looking at me.

"Isaac?" I asked timidly.

He nodded and said, "He's gone. I'm the new landlord. Do you need help with anything?"

"Nope!" I said and rushed away from that place in a shock.

I felt terrible about what happened with Isaac the other day. I think that he probably tried to let me know that he was moving out. He probably got lucky with his freelancing job and finally got a break in Hollywood, but I wouldn't know that because I messed up big time. I never got to share my own incredible story with him.

2.

Welcome to the Land O' Meaning

"As the man threw the seeds, they were cast forth by a mysterious wind. Next thing I knew there was a germination process taking place."

This story unfolds in the year 1980 when students all over the nation had to be a part of a mandatory "Literacy Campaign." Personally, I think it was one of the most noble causes in which I had ever participated. We helped our most vulnerable people to learn how to read and write, and we were trained and educated to be a part of the mission. My group was assigned to a breathtaking and unknown region in a city called Jinotega. When we arrived, after so many hours of traveling, we still had to hike far and wide into the wild and in and out of mountains, towns, villages, and virgin jungles. I started to live an awesome life in the wild (a guy's dream) amongst monkeys, deer, coyotes, and mountain lions.

Nicaragua is about the size of New York State and is divided into fifteen departments (some small and some large counties). We have two regions, which are still mostly virgin lands, and many indigenous people remaining there called **Miskitos.** They used to live very primitively and in very precarious conditions back in the day.

These Native Americans were a mix of runaway African slaves who either escaped from the hands of slave traders, sinking boats, or from nearby islands. They were also descendants of English pirates. The village we arrived at was named *San José del Bocay.* When we arrived at that part of Jinotega, we thought the jungle was a hostile and infested place filled with wild boars and crocodiles. We still had a day and a half to get to our final destination, a small village named *Aguas Calientes*. It was up north near the border with Honduras.

We marched down through treacherous roads, surrounded by the beauty of lots of rivers and creeks, probably infested with amoebae or poisonous snakes like bushmasters, rattlesnakes and other species of the same kind, and poisonous frogs with beautiful bright colorful skin. We named it *la tierra de nadie* (nobody's land). We also had a saying that "life was worthless" in these lands because, if

18

something serious happened to any of us, like getting severely sick, we weren't going to make it out alive because the closest doctor from us was a long walk away. We quickly learned that many students (brigadistas) died in this mission from infamous snakebites or accidental fatal gunshot wounds while others drowned in the rivers.

There was no electric power or a decent meal to even suppress our hunger. Most peasants only grew poor quality beans and corn. Very few had banana plants, orange groves, or other non-attractive fruits. We were truly disappointed, not good for a city boy expectation. We worried about swimming in any contaminated rivers since we noticed that what seemed to be non-contaminated rivers served as sewage to the villages ahead that had their latrines right on the river. Sometimes we did not know if we've chosen the right spot to sleep at night when we noticed snake nests in the dark.

The worst was about to come. We were also warned about minefields spread out in these mountains as well. We were told stories of people blowing up into hundreds of pieces when they walked in these fields or grabbed a live grenade by mistake. We met many people young and old, with missing limbs, as a result of casualties in some of the towns we passed by to get to our final destination, and that made it very scary. Thank God nothing happened to any of us in my brigade.

Teenagers are not fearful enough; I was one of them then. Yet, I thought I knew it all, that tomorrow would never come, and that I would not die easily. I was going to live forever and die only when I was very old.

Upon arrival there were some soldiers sent to San Jose Del Bocay, Russians and Cubans helping out in this nationalist project. They brought with them some recycled uniforms and boots from their armies. The Russian boots were awesome. Hopefully, they did not take them off their dead army soldiers. I tried to put that thought aside, but I

19

couldn't help to be a clown about it. Many of my friends laughed with me. One Russian soldier gave me a dirty look, but I kept acting like a clown. I couldn't care less what he thought of me. If he didn't have a sense of humor, that was his problem.

At that time we could not be choosy or bitchy. We needed great footwear to last in the mountains. I found a pair that fitted me right. They were a nice reddish/brown color. The obnoxious Russian soldier threw the selections on the ground like we were a bunch of savages.

Unlike the Russian soldier, a Cuban soldier was kind and friendly. He brought about 70 pairs of army uniforms. I only took a pair of pants. I did not have any needs for the long sleeve jacket. It was too sticky and hot to wear one of those, but later I found out that I screwed up really badly because when it rained, it got awfully cold in the ***tropical rainforest,*** and also the jacket protected you from any mosquito bites.

I still made a good choice; the weather didn't bother me at all, regardless. I was one of the few lucky ones to have a pair of those boots that fit my size. I had a chance to pick, choose and try on a few pairs, plus pants, to find the right ones for me. The ones I chose were all the way up to the middle of my calves. I was there at the right moment and at the right time. We were probably around a hundred young men but had only about fifty pairs of Russian army boots. Having to choose your own pair turned into an angry wasp hive. I rushed my way out of there quickly with my top choice.

It took about four more hours driving on a treacherous road with huge abysses on both sides, and rivers that easily could turn a truck upside down because the water currents were either very strong or had many, slippery, big rocks when the trucks drove through those strong currents. Also, some areas were very rainy all the time, or they had huge mud pools and holes in the road everywhere. Although the tires were very tall and strong, the trucks seemed weak and looked as if they were not made with a very strong metal structure. It felt as if the metal would collapse easily.

I was analyzing the whole operation, and it had more holes than a chunk of Swiss cheese. Yet, I kept my thoughts to myself, but I was very eager to help out.

I was praying all the way to the end of the odyssey to make it with my friends in one piece. We finally arrived at this small village called *San Jose del Bocay*. We thought that we were going to end our tour there, but little did we know.

A group leader came along with a cocky personality and said while pointing, "Well in this village, we are placing the females but most of the guys are going to be spread out in those mountains ahead with farming families."

According to that guy, these families were already informed of the literacy campaign coordinators, and that they would feed and care for us as an exchange for our time and dedication in teaching them how to read and write. We would help them work their crops to earn our daily bread. We were also encouraged to help them around with their daily chores. They would teach us if we didn't know how to seed the land.

I kept asking myself how in the world could I do any of that. The only thing I knew about was helping my mom with her plants and only because she paid me a cordoba (Nicaraguan currency) per plant. I knew how to plant and prune rose bushes back home using gloves to protect me from pricking myself with the thorns.

"How would I be able to do anything in the crop fields for God's sake?!" I thought.

I did not want to learn how to stay dirty and stinky all the time. I felt screwed.

I couldn't see myself doing any farming. I was an embarrassment to the program. Me seeding beans, corn, or milking cows? Ridiculous! I had no intention of working my butt off for a plate of food, in this case beans. I could do that for fun but not for the love of farming. I either learned the hard way and got involved, or I died of hunger. So, once we arrived at our destinations, I had to hurry to work in the fields and burn my skin like a poor, shoeless peasant.

Likewise, I literally learned for the first time what the Bible had to say about earning our daily bread: "By the sweat of your face you shall eat bread." In this situation, it was tortillas, the bread of my ancestors, the Mayas. That was an important lesson that helped me along my way to adulthood.

Time past by and I became a master about their techniques. I learned to farm, harvest and guess the weather almost to perfection like a rainy day or a sunny day. I also learned when to harvest corn and beans and pick up tomatoes. I learned to tell time without a clock. As I got used to working hard, I also learned to appreciate the people for their condition and admired them for their love of life. I learned to value their lives even if in my personal opinion they lived in miserable conditions. They had to do that until they died. That wasn't my way of seeing my life, yet I learned to respect them for that.

It came to pass that I learned to live like a peasant. I let myself just drop anywhere and lie down for hours thinking about the great food I used to eat at home or at my grandparents' farm. Grandma's chicken casserole, yummie! I remembered I could still feel the awesome taste in my mouth. I'd kill just to have a cold Coca Cola with ice cubes going down my thirsty throat, or our famous Nicaraguan stir-fried steak and onions with French fries, white rice, and a green salad, hmmm! I then woke up realizing it was all a bad dream, and I was sad the rest of the day.

***

One day months later, an acquaintance from my same brigade, Jorge Espinoza, and I requested permission to go see our folks in Managua. All of a sudden, I fell ill just a few miles down the road in a village called ***El Cuá***. I was probably having an amoeba attack. My symptoms were high fever, throwing up, and a cold sweat constantly. I was also shivering and felt I wasn't gonna make it through the night. I was going to miss all the fun, the adventurous way of going back 150 miles of walking, hitchhiking, and riding public transportation until I got home. Even though we were continuing our journey the next day, I knew that I was in such bad shape that there was no way I could feel better that soon.

Jorge left me lying on the porch of an abandoned, deteriorating home, though the outside porch was in great shape. I remember sinking into a very dark hole and my energy was totally gone. My friend covered me with a blanket, rubbed some mentholated ointment on my back, throat and arms, gave me a lemonade, and fed me a couple of pills for the cold before leaving me in the middle of nowhere, so to speak.

I felt so devastated that I told him, "I think I am dying!"

He smiled and told me to relax and sleep it off. Then he left.

After a while, a bright light hit me on my face and woke me. Someone was rubbing a soft sweet hand on my forehead. For a moment, I thought it was my mom, but then I realized I was in the middle of nowhere. My mom didn't even know where I was. I slowly opened my eyelids trying to figure it out. I was bothered by the light on my eyes, although pleasant at the same time, just like a warm summer breeze.

What I saw before me was a silhouette of a female being leaning towards me, a beautiful, mysterious lady. She then crouched down on the wooden stairs just to meet me face to face. I thought her face looked familiar, but I couldn't remember from where. The woman was dressed like an Ancient Greek goddess with an illuminated aura all over her. She wore white clothing, a shawl and had very long hair. She did shine very strongly when she appeared before me.

My sickness disappeared after that lady rubbed her hand across my forehead. I was still weak as a result of the fever, yet quite awake then. I had not eaten anything during the whole day. The lady smiled and offered me some soup that tasted like chicken and mint. I still had issues with my throat; it felt as if it were burning inside. I looked at the time on my Seiko watch: 7 PM. I drank the broth, and just like magic, my throat soothed and healed almost immediately. I thanked the nice lady and felt the need to go back to sleep again. Then, she vanished!

A while later, Jorge came holding some soup in his hand, and his face was all happy. He asked me to wake up and drink some of the broth, but I wasn't hungry any longer. I looked at the time on my wristwatch and it was 9:03 PM,

"That's impossible!" I thought.

I shared my story with him about some beautiful but odd-looking lady who already had fed me something to eat. He couldn't care less about my story, so he decided to drink the soup himself. I sweated from the fever and had the need to get back to sleep only this time with a smile on my face.

***

Later back in Managua, my parents took me to restaurants and fed me well enough to last me another few months in those inhospitable lands. Then, I was back with my friendly, but very poor adoptive family in the mountains. I remember I worked so hard in the fields. I remember telling Pedro (the dad in the family) I was having problems with my vision, and somehow, I blamed the sun being so strong and hot more than usual, so he let me go and take a break. I went to the cornfields and lay there for a while. I didn't care about mountain lions, coyotes, or poisonous snakes; I just dropped myself on the ground like a bag of potatoes under a tree with a nice shadow.

Welcome to the Land O' Meaning

All of a sudden, a tingling feeling covered me all around my body when a very bright light shone upon my face. I woke up to find out something scary was crawling on top of my chest and I freaked out. I grabbed it and threw it away from me. It was a nasty black poisonous snake.

I then got up and to my amazement I was in this beautiful and perfect field, not the cornfields, but a wheat field. I walked around it. The sky was colorful in its own splendor of blues, and there were a few clouds. The blue was very pleasant to my eyes, and the wheat brightened up with a golden color. The snake was a dead branch that broke off and fell on top of my waist.

I came to an understanding that I was not where I was supposed to be. I was somewhere else and saw that very clean little people were working those fields. I wondered how that could be as I never had seen them before.

"What in the world has just happened to me?" I asked myself.

"Welcome to the Land O' Meaning!" is how I was greeted by a handful of friendly little men. When they touched my hands, I became peaceful and aware of all knowledge, and my mind opened up.

It seemed like everyone knew what I was doing there. They all smiled at me. Usually farmers in that part of the world were shy, their skin was darkened by the sun, and they resembled their Indian ancestors. They had lean bodies with a lot of muscles, and usually they smelled like wet sweat. Most of the time, they had dirty clothes on, because of their harsh work in the mud, or just for being near the raw ground all the time. Their hands were also very rough.

Not these people.

They had their farmer's working clothes on, but very bright, clean, unblemished, white cotton. They did not smell like sweat at all. Their hair was red, abundant and hung down to their cheeks. Their eyes were blue, very blue like the color of a clear sky. I couldn't believe they were peasants. But they were working the land. Their hands did not have any signs of roughness; their fingernails were very clean and clear. It did not make any sense; the sun did not tan their skin tone as they had pale skin. Nothing made sense in my head anymore.

Their stature was shorter than all the peasants I knew in the area. I was considered a tall boy to those locals at 5'6" height then. Usually, they were smaller but by a couple of inches. Yet these people were shorter by far (small like children but they looked like grown-ups). The tallest was maybe 4'6". They had no sign of wrinkles or showed any signs of sickness like the poor peasants I knew who usually did not look so healthy. Most of the peasant kids seemed weak, unlike these children. They were healthy and cheerful. Every one of them was putting in their share of work. They all worked together in harmony like a real team and seemed like a real family.

***

These little people were unlike the peasants I knew.

For example, the head of the peasant family, the father, worked to death in the field by himself. Off and on, he'd get someone to help him because sometimes the work was extremely harsh. This time I was that helping hand.

The peasant wife took care of the household duties like washing the clothes every day in the river, scrubbing the mud and dirt right off on the river stones and rocks. The children were always with her while she worked on her daily chores.

Later, she cooked their meal, usually boiled beans with a lot of salt, and she manually chopped the wood with an ax. I tried once to help her, and she laughed her head off when I couldn't retrieve the ax after my first intent to chop some wood. We both laughed, and she then taught me the tricks. I learned and got myself a pair of rough hands full of splinters by chopping her wood every now and then. Next, she used her hands to manipulate the corn dough to prepare tortillas.

The lady used a pair of stones to grind the boiled corn, a flat stone that laid at the bottom and a round long stone to manipulate the dried boiled kernels. Then, she turned that into corn dough and into giant tortillas with fragments of the kernels' shells because she didn't have a filter to get rid of them. So, the lint (product of the shells) got stuck in our throats until we coughed them all out throughout the day of work. That was the only thing I could not learn how to deal with.

***

In contrast, my experience with the little red-haired people was completely different.

They had many communities in the fields. I was in a section where at least seven homes and families related to each other embraced my arrival and took me in as their guest. I could see in the distance other communities though they didn't intrude while I was visiting. The community that I was in had no more than fifty members.

They talked to me in a strange language with sounds I had never heard before, but I did understand what they meant when they addressed me. They would open their mouths, speak words, and thoughts came into my ears. The same thing happened to me when I talked back to them, and it felt natural. I can't say they spoke my language, yet I felt that we had a good understanding of each other. They treated me like family, like one of them coming from a different realm, yet as if they were expecting me as a normal event and not as if I just appeared out of the blue as I thought I did.

They invited me to their outdoor long wooden table with white linen and a beautiful finish. Flowers, fruits and stocks of wheat decorated the table. Food was aplenty. The table seemed to have no more than twenty seating places on

27

benches. I was with a family of perhaps seven members plus myself.

They set a platter of tortillas in the center of the table. The platter was made of red clay. They placed giant, refined tortillas made of wheat without the lint on the platter. I never had such good flavor before in my life. They put another platter with some sort of meat that tasted like rare veggies and meat, and a jug of fresh milk better than any milk I've ever had before in my life.

Reflecting on the experience, we never actually spoke with our lips. I just followed along and didn't feel the need to question anything. The sounds came into my head strangely enough. I did understand with my brain but not with my human logic. They only smiled and pointed at things. I never felt motivated to speak to them with my mouth either.

I had to be dreaming. No one in this area lived like they do. They all cooperated and came together to the table. That was too much. The people back home I knew lacked common courtesy. Although they were very nice, they did not have any sophisticated manners.

***

After we ate, they showed me how to improve the soil to prepare it for the harvest, and without any spoken words I learned a few tricks. Although the elder farmer was dressed in all white, he never got dirty nor showed any signs of sweating.

This little man grabbed a bag of seeds, spat on them, and threw them on an empty field. Every time he did that, he talked to them and blessed them.

"Bring forth a great harvest in these fields to feed my family and plenty enough to share with our friends," he said.

As the man threw the seeds, they were cast forth by a mysterious wind. They ended up all over the gray dirt. The fields immediately got wet and the seeds sank in. Next thing I knew there was a germination process taking place. The old man smiled at me and told me not to lose hope.

I observed that the natural elements of wind, fire and water acted upon their request, not as magic, but more like in perfect harmony. The intriguing part was that these natural elements seemed to have a soul or spirit within them as if they were alive and connected to these people.

The old man further taught me that in my dimension we were designed to work hard for anything that our bodies and dreams desired or wished for, and so we needed to embrace our fate. I also learned that our consciousness would always have needs that were not healthy like vanity, ego, pride, selfishness, etc. And that was what made the world we know so unstable because we were not following the way to harmony but to wickedness and darkness. We had lost our direction and were bound to our fate unless we learned to let go and be more giving without expectations of any kind.

The secret is to find the gift of true happiness within ourselves. Therefore, we would radiate positive energy to our brethren instead of pushing them away and making them feel that they're nothing but a bunch of losers and have nothing to share with the world.

***

They patted my back and sent me back to where I came from. I noticed they sent the smallest child to walk me to a very specific spot where I remember the whole thing came to be. As we walked back, I noticed a white horse, a white dog, a white goose, and white birds flying in the sky. I was also wearing a white shirt and white pants. I had no shoes on, and I saw that the little people's feet were bare as well.

I reflected on the mysterious woman in white who weeks earlier had served me a healing broth while I lay sick on that abandoned porch and wondered if she was one of the little people. Yet, I did not see her among them. Instead, I think that she was more like an angel, a healer, or a guardian of the truth. I was on a mission to learn from the little people and share those lessons with the world as I'm now doing in this story. She helped me to recover to fulfill that mission!

I did not see the separation of land parcels where I came from. It was a distant, rich farming area with all the little people working for the same purpose.

When I arrived home, the first thing I felt was the awful odor of my own sweat. I wanted to run and jump into the river and take a bath, but I felt so exhausted. I felt like I had been working hard all day.

I saw Pedro coming towards me.

"We were worried sick about you. We had not seen you since yesterday afternoon!" he said.

To my surprise, I tried to figure that out, but they did not understand my questioning. They went around in circles with the story.

All I remember saying was, "Don't worry about me. I was around."

***

A thought of remembrance entered my mind the first day we arrived at **San Jose Del Bocay**. I remember I saw a mountain at a distance, and I liked mountains. I asked a local how long would it take me to walk up to that mountain. I remember his expression was of disbelief.

He said to me, "I wouldn't recommend any of you make any trips to that mountain. It's bewitched. It's called **The Leprechaun's Mountain**. Little people are said to kidnap anyone who dares to explore it!"

The next morning, a group of friends and I went straight to that mountain, and we found a small cave. There were two red hands painted on the wall in the entrance, and we found weird pots and a big eye made of stone, but we didn't

30

experience any paranormal activity there. Besides that, it was kind of creepy.

These remains had nothing to do with the little people, yet the locals believed the little people appear and disappear in that area. I also believe that area was a portal to their dimension and a sacred place for my Mayan ancestors while they lived in these lands and were in harmony with Mother Nature!

After my experience with the little, red-haired people, I had a great smile on my face the rest of the whole campaign. I had food for thought that was going to last me for a while in my mind. I had met people that were not from this plane of life, and I learned that there are ways to live a better life and that it was possible to live in harmony. I remember only a little bit about my conversation with these little people. But what I do remember remained with me to this day.

"It's gonna get better for you, be good!"

3.

The Creepy Old Man with the Christmas Bell

"When I got up, to my horror the creepy old man
from downtown Managua was there in flesh and blood!"

Every weekend my folks had a plan, and I was included since I was the youngest of my siblings. Sometimes we went to the movies or visited relatives. Christmas holidays were right around the corner. In the past we had visited one of my dad's best friends and longtime colleagues Ricky Barbosa. They lived in the outskirts of Managua; it was called *Carretera Sur* (or South Road). They had a nice city farm just a few blocks off the main road towards *Las Nubes* (The Clouds). It is a real cold area where there is a lot of temperature changes in weather, sometimes dropping quickly and making it chilly all of a sudden. We always packed sweaters when we drove to that area. Only that day, my dad decided to go visit them without a plan.

The Barbosas' home had a name, *La Tabulla* (rope made of plant fibers). My folks had known them forever, and they had visited our home as well. I liked farms and hills because it reminded me of my grandmother's farm, a place where I was tremendously happy. Plus, I loved nature and animals. We also took Sultan, our German Shepherd dog. He was yellow, white and black. That way I could run and play with him and scream all I wanted. No one would be supervising or bothering me. But before visiting Ricky, we went to downtown Managua, had lunch there, and ran some Christmas errands.

At a corner on *Avenida Roosevelt,* there was a Santa Claus, year after year for the whole month of December. Santa was always giving children some candies. This time was not different. He was greeting children and ringing his bell with a funny look on his face and a jolly laugh. I begged my dad to stop and let me greet Papa Noel, a fun thing to do around the holidays. I was a hundred percent positive he was the real thing regardless of what other kids at school had told me. Dad stopped with a big smile on his face. They let me out of the car to run to the jolly fat man with the white beard like all the other kids surrounding him. I was acting a little shy, but I did not mind greeting him and shaking his hand.

"Hello, Santa," I simply said.

He smiled but wasn't looking at me.

I still hugged him dearly.

You can be a kid, but you notice when things are weird. He was looking through me, but not at me.

I kept saying "Hello, Santa Claus."

I was this naïve and innocent boy. All he did was breathe heavily and kept looking right through me. I noticed that he stared at my folks and my dog, but not at me or at the other kids.

The other folks that were around Father Christmas were trying to take a snapshot, but it was difficult because there were too many kids. Back in those days, people used the 35mm Agfa Camera with the disposable purple flash for every take.

Santa had this big bag of toys. The toys were cheap and made of plastic. He also had cheap candies like lollipops and other hard candy that probably were to promote the toy company right at that corner where he was standing. The beautiful, decorated lights and stores made the scenery pleasant and very attractive for everyone.

Santa's white gloves were kind of tearing off, and I could see part of his hand. His skin was orange, very tangy. Then his glove came off from all the pulling and pushing of the kids around him, exposing the fingers of his right hand. They looked creepy. He had large fingernails. They were sharp and dirty. When I realized all that, he caught me off guard and stared me in the eyes. At that moment, I felt the need to run away from his grip. He wasn't smiling anymore. He had a cheap plastic car toy in his hand. He would give it away to whomever got close to him. So, I grabbed it and fought with him for a few seconds. His smile turned unfriendly followed by a creepy sounding grunt. I broke off the back wheels of the cheap toy car and tried to run like there was no tomorrow, but he was still holding on to the toy. When I got loose from his control, I escaped and did not go back for whatever had fallen on the ground. I just wanted the heck out of there and got into my dad's car breathing heavily. As I looked back, the creepy old man was still staring at me.

"Why couldn't adults see what I saw?" I wondered.

My folks were smiling with their minds somewhere else, but Sultan kept barking angrily at the old man, yet no one noticed anything strange.

"Did you have a good time, champion?" said my dad smiling.

My only response was "Hmm, yeah!"

I did not sound so convincing, but adults do not want to deal with it. I did not want to sound like a crybaby, so I left it at that. I remember I threw whatever was left of the plastic toy under my dad's seat and even kicked it, so I did not have to see it anymore. I hated that darn toy.

We continued our trip to Ricky's home. I was usually at the window letting the air blow through my hair and hands, but this time, I did not feel like myself, so I just wanted to let it go unnoticed. We finally made it to **La Tabulla**.

My dad parked, and I jumped out of the car. Sultan followed along with me barking and jumping. He made me forget my awful struggle. I greeted Ricky and his wife Gemina, and we left to the side of a hilltop and played ball for a while. We also chased some small farm animals; we loved to do that all the time. I'd forgotten all about the creepy old man. I could hear my folks and their friends playing some music and dancing, and they were having cold beers and finger foods. I went for some of the finger goodies and fed Sultan tiny meatballs and sausage on toothpicks. Sultan certainly appreciated it.

When we went back to the hills, Sultan suddenly started to bark angrily at something. I tried to see what it was but couldn't see a thing. Then I saw him rushing after a fox, and there was no way I could stop him from chasing the frightened animal. I chased after him and went all the way down the mountain to see if I could convince my dog to follow me and keep playing with me, but I couldn't even hear his barks anymore. So, I went to my dad and told him what happened, but he did not seem bothered.

"When we are ready to go, Sultan is going to show up, you'll see," was all he said.

I didn't care anymore. I began to roll down the hilltop as the tall grass was very green and soft to play safe. I did roll over for some time until I hit a bumpy ride. I felt I hit something man made. When I got up, to my horror the creepy old man from downtown Managua was there in flesh and blood!

I rubbed my hands over my bug eyes to see if I was hallucinating.

Getting up, I asked him, "What are you doing here, mister?"

In my mind I couldn't realize how he knew where we were or how did he even know *La Tabulla*? I had no logical explanation, but he was there not answering. His face was fixed on me. He then grabbed onto me as if I was an object, and I felt his nails cutting through my skin like sharp knives. I fought him and defended myself by kicking at him for a while. It was so frightening that I couldn't scream. I knew this was not a normal situation and something was wrong with the picture, but I did not know how to perceive it at that very young age.

All of a sudden, my dog Sultan came to my rescue and barked at him out of nowhere.

"Good boy," I said.

The creepy man yelled like a hurt wild animal, and I managed to get away from his ugly hands and grip. He couldn't chase me any more while my dog kept barking madly at him. I ran back to the house and made it to my folks, and they noticed me hurting. I tried to explain myself, but they did not care about what I had to say. I kept saying "Santa," but they couldn't make any sense out of it. They thought I got hurt playing.

I stood up firmly and said, "He told me I was a bad seed."

Gemina yelled angrily, "Who called my boy a bad seed?"

But she was being playful, and they all had a silly smile on their faces and forgot all about it. The party continued. She placed a bandage on the side of my belly where I had a scratch and that was it.

Minutes later at some distance, there he was! Creepy Santa Claus walked by dragging his heavy boots. He stared at me making it out of the property, and no one even bothered to look at him.

"How is it that I was the only one seeing these awful things?" I thought to myself.

The afternoon turned into night, and it was time to leave. Dad was a bit tipsy from all the alcohol he consumed. There was only one way out of *La Tabulla*, and it was kind of dark already. As we left, the creepy old Santa sat there on a bus bench on the road right under an old light pole barely lit and surrounded by this white mist because the temperature had dropped and got very cold suddenly. The creepy old man stared at me with a stupid, silly look on his face. Sultan barked at him some more, but no one even cared. I've always tried to deny that experience, so I've called it a nightmare ever since.

We finally arrived home and dad went straight to bed. Mom read a few of her fashion magazines in the living room. I went to watch a late TV show with my other brothers.

Mom said to us, "This is your last show kids. After this, you gentlemen go to bed."

We complained, but she was the boss back then. Then I heard the bell ringing at a distance. I looked around and my brothers had split. I looked at my mom, and she had fallen asleep reading her magazines, so I went to the closest window and saw the creepy old man ringing the Christmas bell on the corner outside my home. The odd thing was that no one was around him. He gazed and saw me watching him.

He smiled making that awful sound he was doing in downtown.

Later, I felt that he grabbed my foot, but when I screamed, I woke up. I was sound asleep in my own bed. It was horrible. Everyone was asleep, and I got up and went to the same window in my dream. Since I was small and younger, I pushed a chair towards the edge of the window, stood up, and saw a very dense mist under the pole. Usually back in those days, there was some kind of mist that is no longer a part of our weather. This time was no exception. I heard clearly and loudly that noise the creepy man made with his heavy breathing. His hand moved with the motion of the bell, but I couldn't hear the sound of the bell. As my eyes popped wide open and kept seeing part of his expression and motion, I grabbed my favorite blanket and rushed into my bed. I had a cat named Miss Fuzz. She was there sleeping with me, and I grabbed onto the cat and forced myself to sleep. Thank God it was just a dream.

***

Days passed by, and I did not see Santa Creepy Clause any more. I always stayed alert for that fetid smell that came from his clothing. It was a mixture of old vinegar and sulfur, like those chemicals that are used for cleaning around the house, and I just tried to avoid at all cost.

It was customary that kids for Christmas season write letters to baby Jesus to get their presents, but the one who deliver them was Santa Claus according to Nicaraguan tradition. I wasn't sure I wanted Santa to take my letter any longer, so I asked my dad how can I do that without having Santa involved. Dad told me to place my letter behind a picture of the Holy Sacred Heart of Jesus that hung on the middle of our living room wall.

Days later, I did. I placed my wish note behind the Jesus picture that night.

My dad called me and asked me if I wrote that card myself and I replied with a simple, "Yes."

"What in the world were you thinking of?" asked my dad.

He went on to explain to me the ridiculous details of the letter and was really upset because of a cruel joke drawn on it. I made an effort to remember what happened on that day. I did recall that I was sitting with the other kids from around the block, and all of us were writing our cards together. After that, I went home as fast as I could to deliver the wish letter when I tripped on something and my letter flew away from my hands. A passerby picked it up and handed it back to me. He was a fat, short, stinky man. I remember wondering why did he smell like that creepy Santa from downtown? He smelled really bad and had an awful smile, with sharp teeth and a heavy breathing, and his fingernails were dirty, long, and sharp.

"Here, boy," the man said staring at me from head to toe.

He frightened me a bit and reminded me of that evening at the Barbosas' home. So, I rushed back into my house and said nothing to him. He was still breathing heavily. I didn't look back. I remember placing my card behind the picture and forgot all about it. I asked dad why he was asking me if I wrote the letter. He handed me the card so I could see for myself. There was a morbid drawing of a boy hanging from a rope and an unsuspected hand with a bloody knife stabbing the boy as he hung from the rope. I complained immediately that it wasn't what I had written on it. Yet, the only word on the letter was a title, which read **La Tabulla**, and at the bottom my name was signed exactly the way as I used to write my name. My dad had a disappointed expression as if I were part of that cruel joke when I wasn't. He then ripped up the letter and threw it into the garbage. He was very upset about the whole thing. I fished it out of the garbage can and gave it another look. I had a flash back in my mind about the creepy old man's heavy breathing and his bell ringing. I was wondering what did all of that mean, but as a boy myself, I did not pay any more attention to that and continued on with my life.

Finally, Christmas arrived on December 24th in Latin America tradition. Mom was across the way in the neighbor's home with dad celebrating adults' Christmas which was smoking cigarettes, eating sausages on toothpicks, with refried beans and tostones (fried plantains), and drinking whiskey. Mom and the other ladies didn't drink hard liquor at those gatherings.

Most neighbors gathered to celebrate while their kids would be sleeping at home waiting for Papa Noel to deliver their Christmas presents. I knew mine were going to be delivered by baby Jesus himself because I had nothing to do with that fat, stinky, old, kook anymore.

My siblings were all asleep. I abruptly woke up from a pleasant dream but couldn't move my whole body except for my eyes. I saw flashing lights all over the house. I knew ghosts since I can remember; evil spirits were more like it. I could never sleep with the disturbance of ugly, old hags dressed in nightgowns invading the living room, their hair all messed up and fuzzy. It was incredible that my siblings were asleep in the house. The evil spirits sounded like they were really upset about something, but no one woke up with all that noise. I was the only one up.

Later, Mom came rushing in. She seemed desperate about something, but everyone was asleep, and I was awake but couldn't move a limb.

My mother was looking around for those same witches or signs of them because she had the same abilities I did. I knew all about them! I see them all the time, but I couldn't get to say anything. I felt so wasted. I was under some evil spell, so I just went straight back to sleep.

The next morning, we all woke up to open up our presents. I took my toys to the front porch out of the house. The creepy Santa Claus was riding a breadman's delivery bike. He had a big wire basket on the front of the bike and riding inside the basket was that very short, fat guy that picked up my Christmas card from the gutter. The fetid odor of dirty cloth soiled in vinegar was spread out all over the neighborhood. They smiled at me with their awful heavy breathing and gave me a military salute.

For a long time after that, I despised Christmas holidays. I was so upset about what happened to me and blamed the jolly old man. I remember potato head (a bully from my neighborhood) came to me with a stupid smirk on his face and asked me if I believed in Santa Claus. I looked up at the sky and saw his sleigh with reindeer and bells ringing, followed by a cloud of sparkling dust left in their path until they disappeared into the clouds.

I said to him, "Not anymore!"

Suddenly, I woke up from another terrible dream to the sound of creepy Santa Claus' bell and his fetid smell.

***

Looking back, the reason for this experience was to show me that it has always been the job of evil spirits to destroy or provoke death on sensible souls who can see evil's true form. My gift was that I could see this creepy Santa's real intention beyond the veil. He was using a Santa disguise to lure innocent souls like me into his web and corrupt them slowly but surely over time to the dark side. Then, these dark souls could spread evil throughout the world.

Even his fat sidekick riding in the bicycle basket was in on the ruse.

When this creepy Santa saw that I knew who he really was and could expose him to everyone, he pursued me in a diabolical way to drive me crazy and finally submit to him. That's why he appeared in the field at the Barbosas' home and later across the street from our house ringing his Christmas bell. All to drive me insane. Or if not, to cause me great injury or death. Hence, the crude drawing of the hanging boy being stabbed mysteriously appeared in the Santa letter. I confess that I must have drawn it but totally suppressed the memory due to a paralyzing fear.

The old hags and witches that I saw, and my mom felt in the house, appeared after being greatly agitated by the presence of the creepy Santa who was both taunting me in the real plane as well as in my dreams which always became nightmares.

Luckily, I always have my Guardians to protect me from such evil. I do not know where they come from, but I sense that they are always there watching over me. Yes, I could say that my Guardians are archangels and angels from the etheric dimensions. I do pray for their protection and feel that my prayers are answered.

The rest of the world is asleep to all of this paranormal activity going on, and no one even cares to even acknowledge it. It is not a part of what humanity considers true reality but rather a figment of a traumatized, weak human. The world is full of mysteries and incredible stuff like this, but we are programmed to see only in one direction. Otherwise, we're considered a clinical case and a person with little or no credibility.

4.

The Devil Attacks

"There he was, I saw him. I was face to face
with the source of all-evil, the DEVIL himself."

When I was a small boy, I had my doubts about the devil they preached at mass or in my Sunday school class. I learned not to trust most adults for many reasons. I caught them at a very early age lying or withholding the truth for their convenience. That included my siblings, my educators, and even my own folks.

Since then I have encountered many paranormal experiences. Sometimes I didn't know if I had encountered angels or demons. The demons were so deceiving. To be honest, I couldn't put my finger on it: whether to call them a divine intervention or an evil one like poltergeists. Now that I am a grown-up, my first recollection of events that I can remember without going under hypnotherapy were ghostly figures that I saw on the TV screen at night when everyone was asleep, and the TV set was turned off. Often in the daytime, I also heard voices calling my name in the distance.

Time passed, and my intuition about the paranormal was making me aware of many things. I had a lot of issues with people, because I could sense their intentions and couldn't deal with it. I still haven't figured out how to control these experiences. They come and go as they wish.

Between 2000 through 2010 my psychic abilities were bombarding me with information, dreams, visions, and more of the paranormal abductions, ghosts, possessions, messages and vivid dreams, etc. These years were the worst time of my life and my downfall. I had this spiritual battle where I was the only one fighting with myself or against demons.

My family had been a family of faith. Everyone had been Catholic. I went to a Catholic school when I was young, and my parents and their parents were devoted Catholics. I was so alone in my spiritual battle that I learned to pray the Holy Rosary on my own. The first day I started praying I was living in Miami, Florida at the time, and my apartment was filled with the essence of roses. Later I found out, one of the Virgin Mary miracles is exactly that. She would fill your surroundings with the awesome smell of roses. Wow, I was perplexed how Mary responded to my prayers. God is with me, I thought to myself, and I was very happy.

On the seventh night that I kept praying the Holy Rosary, I did it to make sure some dark souls that were trying to communicate with me would leave me alone, once and for all. I was intrigued by a trance where I spoke in different tongues, and the languages fulfilled my spirit. It was a pleasant experience for me. When I was finished, I was mesmerized by the essence of rose flowers again. It strongly filled my whole apartment.

In those years, I rented out one of my rooms to a college student named Bob who practiced Buddhism. He usually burned incense when he meditated for hours in his room, but it smelled like weed or another foul smell of wild herbs. So, I figured Bob had arrived home earlier and finally picked a nice scent to meditate with this time. I wondered about Bob being home so early that evening. He usually arrived home a little past 10 PM. My praying experience happened around 9:30 PM. Also, I never heard the apartment door opening. I went to his room and knocked on his door, but there was no response. I decided to open the door regardless and look inside, but he wasn't there. No incense was burning either. Bob definitely had not come home. I didn't know what to make of it.

The next day, I did the same thing; I prayed the Holy Rosary. This time there was no nice smell of roses anywhere. Instead, I went to sleep early, even though I was not sleepy, because I had something to do the next day in the morning. As I was lying down to cover myself with my sheets, I felt something throw me back forcefully onto my bed. I felt two giant hands grabbing me hard by my wrists and knew that was not coming from God. On the contrary, I knew that demons were angry and tried to submit my spirit to their gain.

At that very moment, I knew it was no flesh and blood, because I couldn't gather myself and open my eyes. I was in a trance. I had just turned the lights off and was pinned down to my bed with this violent force. My heart was beating fast. I was fighting this thing that I could not see. I wanted to scream but no sound would come from my throat.

My spirit released words that did not belong to me: "Lord, let me see my adversary."

An electrifying sensation passed through my body, and my left eye slowly opened. I can't explain with actual words the feeling of fear but at the same time of courage.

There he was, I saw him! I was face to face with the source of all-evil, the DEVIL himself. The hairs prickled on the back of my neck, and I had the sensation of having my heart in my throat.

I anxiously scanned his face in detail like a laser. The beast was a monster probably around nine feet tall. His whole image was translucent, but it had physical strength. I saw it and felt it. He did have a brilliant halo all over him, so I could see it clearly in the dark. The hybrid human-monster-dragon was a being of translucent light. Its snake shaped body was floating on top of mine. He was a super being. The hair on his head was very long and floated as astronauts float in outer space, more like in slow motion, and it never fell on his face. His face was the most hideous mask Hollywood could have ever created in the history of horror movies— exactly like a horrible handful of poisonous snakes sticking out of his head. I was a witness of the most abhorrent show on Earth.

The big hands were more like T-Rex claws in the form of human skeleton hands. He had sharp fangs sticking from the roof of his mouth with a horrible expression as if he was ready to burst out with thousands of profanities. His eyes were like angry fire full of hatred.

I couldn't believe what I was seeing. It became an eternity. I open and closed my eyes to see if I was in a nightmare, but I did not wake up to my normal reality. I knew it was happening in that moment and time. Then, the beast pulled closer to me. I smelled his dragon breath, like warm rotten cow's dung. I tried to kick him, or punch him, but my arms were pinned to the bed where he overpowered me physically but not mentally. No matter how hard I tried to fight him, or kick him, there was some sort of a magnetic field and a specific distance between us such that my feet froze in midair, making it impossible to defend myself from such a beast. I was under his control.

When I was about to give up, he looked at me straight in the eye, and got closer, face-to-face. The smell got worse like a toxic substance. His facial expression seemed a hundred times bigger than that of a human. I also saw all his teeth and they were "pointy." His tongue smelled fetid and it was of purplish color and long. He moved it around like a real snake and sprayed his humor on my face.

Then, he said to me very clearly with a low, beast-sounding voice, "Tí-Te-Re" (in Spanish, which means Puppet). The word is "Títere," but he broke the word into three syllables to make sure it stuck in my head. He meant many things; my mind understood his intentions.

However, for some unexplained reason at that very moment some wisdom came to me. It made me feel very peaceful in my heart and mind, regardless of my agony. I felt safe.

My understanding was, "If he is there in front of me attacking me, be glad because I'm on the right path. Do not fear."

I then blacked out peacefully with a smile on my face.

***

The next morning, I jumped out of bed. I was exhausted. It was a horrible experience, worse than seeing aliens. At least aliens are real creatures, but the one in front of me the prior night was a thing that can only come from what the Church calls "HELL." I had never believed there was such a

47

thing as the Devil. I thought it was a fantasy that religions had made up to keep us on a tight leash. With this experience, I wanted to make sure that everyone knew that the enemy is not your neighbor or another human. The enemy is next to you, and it is a big bad monster. It is as real as the sun, the moon and the stars. He's the dark prince of this world and would hate you if you sought or tried to obey God.

Out of all my experiences ever, this one, was the most real, the most vivid, the clearest. I was fully awake and alert. No one in this world can tell me that my mind made up this story. No one can convince me that it wasn't real. No one has the authority to get in my face and call me crazy or a lunatic for what I've just shared. I can't ever be more certain of that agonizing moment I lived through.

After that experience, I am not afraid of anything evil that is spiritual anymore. I am more afraid of human flesh that lets the enemy take control of their lives.

5.

You Have a Great Gift, Boy

"She was not the first one
who made that sort of comment to me."

By the time I was 12 years old, I saw all kinds of evil spirits, ghosts, strange animals, and such. I had a hard time putting my experiences to words because most of them went beyond my own comprehension. I'd always been afraid to be judged for my hallucinations, premonitions, dreams, or whatever anyone wanted to call these phenomena. To me, all of it was so real and so tangible. I had no doubt I experienced everything in my own skin. During my lifetime I tried to dissect each one of my experiences in order to understand the purpose and reason behind them. Why was I chosen to walk through this path? Throughout all these years, I had considered myself just a simple, ordinary guy, with small dreams and yet, life had always led me to countless extraordinary events.

In the summer of 1974, these infinite experiences remained in my memory. Specific days most of the time became very clear in my mind as if I lived through them yesterday. I had so many experiences to keep up with.

I had a dad who was such a clown. He'd make fun of me, but I couldn't care less what he thought of me or the people around me. My dad used to make fun of anyone, even of himself (although never in my case), unless I screamed in the middle of night claiming I've been taken into space or an evil spirit was trying to make contact with my own spirit. He thought I was making up tall tales, but he never lost his cool about it. I couldn't blame the guy; I would've thought the same thing if someone would make such claims. If I hadn't experienced them myself in my very own skin, I wouldn't have believed them either.

Mom was a firm believer in the God of Israel. She taught us how to pray and trust The Almighty, and that's what I did every time I had an encounter with the unknown. My dad, I think, did not want to know any details about my crazy stories because it was too much for him to handle. He was a down-to-earth kind of man. In other words, he tried to fit into a world where the unknown or the spiritual were considered

50

only for lunatics. So, he always made sure we rolled with what the world expected of us. I didn't agree, but that was the way it was written in his book.

Later on in life, mom confessed that dad had a couple of paranormal experiences himself. So perhaps that was one of the reasons he was acting skeptical all the time. I don't blame him, now that I am older. I can see how hard it is for adults to accept such claims. If I could describe my experiences, I would say that my nights would vary often. I wasn't even trying to tap into my psychic abilities when I began to read people's minds, and I successfully did. I learned a lot about people from their thoughts, and for their intimate desires. I was getting more involved with the unknown and into the unethical.

Sometimes I felt like a thief. Let me rephrase that—I was an invader of people's privacy or dark secrets. I was tapping into something that felt wrong and forbidden. I was snooping into people's lives, and with this, I was getting mixed up with the evil inside of me. It is hard to explain, but the more I tried to find out things about others, the more I was getting addicted to the wrong ideas, and the wrong choices.

During my childhood, I remember starting to get curious about "SEX." Back then, anything related to sex was considered taboo, and I learned quickly most people's true desires and intentions were based on sex. Most people related to an infamous act of sex not necessarily to help populate the world but only to have fun and be promiscuous. I still did not get it in my head; I wanted to know what all of that meant. Anything at all related or not to sex would alert me in such a way that I felt a beast needed to be released from within me.

More often than not, I felt like a hungry beast in the wild, but in my case, I was hungry for the forbidden fruit. It became my new thing, although I did not understand it yet. My body was becoming out of control, and I was afraid of myself. Thank God when I turned thirteen years old, we had our first sexual education class at school. They showed us a film about sexual transmitted diseases. That alone put an end to my uncontrollable sex drive. After a very traumatic experience in class, I definitely scratched sex out of my to-do list. I calmed down and tried to never think about it again.

Visions of future events and paranormal hallucinations came to me unwillingly, just like any ordinary and physiological need. You just knew it. Some spiritual mediums or self-proclaimed seers would walk up to me trying to initiate me into their rituals. It happened to me nearby in the local cemetery. They told me that I made a good medium for their purpose, and that I was a strong magnet for the dead.

A witch once offered me a good remuneration if I accepted working in partnership with her to call out spirits of the dead. I was curious, but I was also concerned and scared to death. I told her I was going to think about it just to avoid the subject. But I always ran the other way when I saw her walking towards me. I was afraid despite my daily battles against evil.

Going back to the day I met that strange witch, it was the same day that I lost my mom's white gold chain covered in diamond dust. My dad gave it to her on their nineteenth wedding anniversary. I always had a thing for fine metals—gold, silver, and stones—real ones. So, when mom did not use her beautiful gold necklace, I would "borrow" it without letting her know I was taking it to school. I went to a private school back then. I knew no one would jump me for it.

Fridays we had sports practice at school, and I wore the shiny gold chain around my neck as usual for all to see. My friend Martina was not happy about it and called me a show off. I wouldn't listen to her, but still took it off my neck for a while and put it inside a pocket in my shorts. I felt it would be safe inside there while I did my soccer practice. By the time PE was over, I had forgotten all about the charming necklace. I went home and soon learned that my mom had plans with my dad that night. They were going out, and my dad asked her to wear her beautiful necklace.

From what I gathered, they were going to a nice event, some musical at the Ruben Dario Theater in downtown Managua, and then they were going to dine in a fancy restaurant, *Los Ranchos,* with some friends, The Avalos. I overheard my mom talking about it on the phone with an old friend, Rocio. She proudly mentioned her shiny, diamond dust, gold necklace Dad gave her as a present for their wedding anniversary. Meanwhile, I was shaking like a leaf because officially I was in deep trouble.

"Darn it," was the last thing I remembered.

I had it in a pocket in my shorts, so I went to my room, got my schoolbag, and looked for that thing without any luck. I turned it inside out, and nothing. I looked back into the schoolbag over and over but found nothing.

So, I thought to myself, "Maybe I never took the necklace in the first place, and perhaps it was all a dream. I dreamt all of it up."

I went into Mom's safe box. She did not know that my siblings all knew the combination code: two digital knobs and three twists to the right stopping at number 25, and two to the left stopping at 26, then counter clockwise to zero and "click," it was safely opened. Gee, we still remember that combination after all these years.

Anyhow, I opened the darn box and everything of value my mom owned was in there but not her new, shiny necklace. I was guilty as sin. Mom knew I loved to wear their gold and silver chains, and both she and my dad kept warning me not to do it. One day, as a matter of fact, I was gonna get it, they said, if I lose any of them.

I started to sweat bullets and was very worried. I knew I'd lost it at school because my peers' response to that was to apply The Law of Finders-Keepers. So that afternoon all I could do was walk desperately around the block trying to make up an excuse for my irresponsible actions. As I walked by Mrs. Aguilar's home in our neighborhood, I heard someone calling me.

"Sh-hhh-sh, boy, come here."

She had a son, Alvaro, my age, and we used to hang out together.

Mrs. Aguilar had a weird smirk on her face as if she was trying to keep from laughing.

Then she said to me, "I need you to do me a favor. I know a witch who comes around the neighborhood every Friday. She reads the Tarot cards to other neighbors, and they claim she's the real thing."

She went on explaining that she wanted to test her abilities to see if she was as good as people claim she was.

"A real witch?" I asked her.

"Yeah!" she replied.

I wonder why she was getting me involved in her nonsense. Mrs. Aguilar was very sneaky with other people, but she was always cool with me, so I listened to her foolish plan.

"What do you need me to do, Mrs. Aguilar?" I asked reluctantly.

"When that witch gets here, you need to pretend that you're minding your own business as you pass by my house. I will pretend to call a stranger, in this case you, but you also need to pretend that you don't know me," she said.

She also made sure to explain that she was going to promote the witch's business by offering to read my palm for a small price to pay, and that I needed to accept. The fee for a reading was only five córdobas (a little less than a US dollar back in those days). She also instructed me to ask the witch any foolish question and to make sure that I was making up a story, just to see what the poor old witch had to say. If the old hag spoke the truth, Mrs. Aguilar assured me that she would pay for my reading.

"Otherwise," she said, "run like hell." She then laughed like hell.

She went on saying that she would tell the old woman that she had never seen me in her life.

I was a bit reluctant about her evil plan.

"What if she chases me and beats me up?" I asked timidly.

Sometimes Mrs. Aguilar could be a troublemaker and somewhat immature for her age. She smiled and kept a funny look on her face.

"She won't. I promise."

At the time Mrs. Aguilar was probably in her late thirties, around my mom's age.

The ruse did happen exactly as she wanted, but with an unexpected twist at the end of the story.

Two things went on in my head at that moment. "Why am I letting her use me for such a childish game?" "Why do I have to accept her deal where I have more to lose and could get in trouble with my parents?"

I tried not to give it a lot of thought. I just wanted to get it over with, and next time, I wouldn't fall again or be a part of her cruel intensions.

So, I was finally ready to trick the old hag, a scary-looking woman, and so I asked her some made up lie. I can't even remember what I said exactly, yet the old woman looked me straight in the eye.

She took a puff of her finger-thin cigar and said to me, "There are many answers to your questions, young sir. But before I answer any of 'em, I would prefer to tell you that there's something more important that is bothering you right now."

At that moment I didn't believe she would say something that would impress me.

So, I said, "What is it, ma'am?"

She took another puff and blew the smoke over my face and firmly said, "You lost something that is very valuable, a jewel that you think is lost forever, something you took without permission. I know where it is; it looks like a necklace, right? So, what do you want to know first?"

I was caught off guard. I never expected such a meaningful response. I did not know what to make of it at that very moment. I didn't know how to face that woman. She was so right. I realized she was talking about the missing necklace—the one I always took as "borrowed," which I needed to find in that precise moment and time. I was in denial.

"Yeah?" I asked. I had no other words for her.

"Your best friend, a girl, (she emphasized) has it. She kept it."

It was incredible for me that she was very detailed and right to the point because usually a boy's best friend is another boy, and I had many best friends, but the one I considered my best friend over all my friends was a girl, my all-time friend Martina Bendaña. How is it that she had it when I knew for a fact that she wasn't even around when I'd lost it? I was in the soccer field playing with my team. Martina wasn't even near that area when I placed the necklace in my pocket.

The old woman repeated, "A friend, a girl, your best friend. Does it ring a bell for you?"

Those words hammered in my head like a nail. Not only did I have no doubts, but that it could not have been a coincidence. The thing was that nobody but me knew what worried me. I had lost that necklace; my mom was going to kill me. I knew for a fact that Martina had nothing to do with the missing necklace. I knew what happened and how I lost it. It was in the field; no one took it from me. I was sure of that!

When I was ready to admit her divination was true, Mrs. Aguilar gestured me to get the hell out, so I did, as I was instructed to respond whether or not the witch was right or wrong.

The gypsy woman quickly said, "I told you the truth, right?"

"I never lost anything, woman! You are nothing but a big liar!" I yelled and started to walk away fast.

She then got very upset.

"You can't go. I'll find you. You must pay me my five córdobas, young man."

I ran like hell and screamed at her something stupid like "burn at the stake, old hag." I was laughing all the way and decided to go meet with my friend Martina. I was in denial but knew the old woman was right. Something in my heart told me that she had a spirit of divination working on her side.

I knocked on Martina's door. There was a window next to the door, and I could see her sitting at her dining table studying.

"Martina," I yelled.

She came to the door with an astonishingly shy smile on her face, totally unlike her. She opened the door.

"What happened to you? What's with that weird look on your face?" I said firmly.

"Nothing. What's up?"

I looked at her straight in the eye.

"Why did you take it, the necklace?"

Deep inside, I doubted she had anything to do with the missing necklace, but I had to risk it. That's all I had left. If the old hag's divination wouldn't work, then I might as well be dead.

"Do you know how much I care for you, and I am about to be confronted by my parents because of it. You've no conscience at all. Why did you do it?"

"Here," she said raising her hand up to my face.

I saw what appeared to be a shy look on her face. I was dumbfounded. For Christ's sake, she took it out of her skirt pocket and handed it to me. I freaked out.

"How in the world?"

Martina explained that she was very upset with me for showing off my mom's expensive jewelry that didn't even belong to me. Previously, she had said that I could lose it and get into real trouble, just like on this occasion. She told me how she was around the soccer field because she had the hots for a boy named Humberto who played on my team. She was there with other girls checking the guy out when she saw me take the necklace and place it in my pocket. As I was in such a rush to start playing, I did not even notice that I'd dropped it on the ground. She stood there among the crowd and picked it up before I kicked it and buried it in the ground.

All she really wanted was to teach me a lesson, so she retrieved it but never intended to keep it for herself. Mystery solved! I was very, very intrigued by that old woman, the fortuneteller's ability to see into the unknown.

***

Days later climbing trees with some friends at the local park, I saw the old witch again taking big drags from a huge cigar. She puffed like an old locomotive. I felt someone was staring at me for a long while as if she knew who I was. I had to admit that I was embarrassed, and I hoped she didn't recognize me from the other day. I was afraid that she would say something about that day when Mrs. Aguilar played her for a fool. I tried to ignore her so maybe she would not recognize me. I thought she was too old and tired to pick a fight.

Time went by, but the old woman kept staring at me, and I couldn't run this time because I had friends I cared about. Gee, if they found out I had ripped off an elderly woman, they would not accept me as one of them. I knew what I did was not acceptable, and my friends would not approve of my behavior. That would've been the end of our friendship. I was very worried. I took my chances and decided to make peace with the old woman. So, I walked up to her and apologized for what happened the other day.

"I knew it was you, the little hoodlum," she said, "but I couldn't be so sure. That's OK, young man, you don't owe me a thing. I knew you were in trouble, so I helped you!"

I did offer to pay back the five córdobas I owed her, although she declined.

"Well, it wasn't my idea but Mrs. Aguilar's in the first place," I responded trying to be funny.

She smiled behind a thick cloud of smoke and said laughingly, "That dishonest woman! I knew it all along! You have a great gift. Don't be afraid to use it, boy!"

Looking down to the ground I asked her, "What do you mean by that, lady?" I was all concerned.

She made references to monsters, ghosts, and visions.

I then left without saying too much. As I turned away from her, I looked back when I was with my friends, and she had left. She had a slow walk in her step and vanished into the distance holding a walking cane.

Her prophetic words led me to believe that I had to practice my abilities since I was curious about the unknown, the hidden, and the mysteries of life. She was not the first one who made that sort of comment to me. I heard it all the time as I was growing up. Psychics or people known as witches in my country and in the USA had said the same thing to me and that I made a good medium for the spiritual world. I got interested. After that encounter with the old woman, I bought myself a **Ouija Board** and with a few kids from around the block, we called up all kinds of spirits. We did not know what we were doing, but I felt the energy taking over my forearms and then my mind. I had rushes in my head and broke into a cold sweat a few times. It was kind of fun, but scary at the same time.

Then, Martina and I saw the movie "The Exorcist." We were at a tender age and not allowed to enter the theaters, but we looked more mature for our years. Martina was a tall girl and that helped. They let us in easy at the Drive-In-Theater. Martina's sister Gabriela and her boyfriend Roger had a Jeep, and we were their chaperons when they dated. The experience was so horrible that I burned the **Ouija Board** right after the movie. I remember we prayed so many Hail Marys and Rosaries for months. I never tried anything stupid again.

***

A few nights later, I had a vision of a black figure, like the shadow of a tall man with a coat rising from beneath my bed, followed by many voices. The voices were clear in my head, and they seemed as if people were calling me. There was a mysterious tapping on my window at night—click, click ...

"Car-loo!" I heard my named being called; I could hear it loud and clear.

I trembled and sweated uncontrollably from my head to my toes and couldn't stop it. All these events started to happen on a daily basis right after my childhood paranormal experiences when I was around six years old at my grandparents' farm. The farm was located only 20 minutes or so away from our home in the city.

Every night was a constant struggle ever since. I had many head rushes of thoughts, ideas, visions, and such. My life was in spiritual chaos from a very early age. After so many constant battles and prayers, another vision came to me, also at night, right after I finished reading my favorite superhero comic books. I saw an older version of our house and was standing there looking through my bedroom window towards the backyard. I then saw what could have been a common "thief" breaking into the house next door to us. He was breaking in through the bathroom upper window. All I could see was the dark, skinny figure of a man.

You Have a Great Gift, Boy

I remember thinking to myself, "My mind is leading me on."

The next day, our neighbor Selma, early 40s, had the worst experience to last her for a lifetime. Her backyard was back to back with ours and divided by a five-foot high concrete fence. Visibility to each other's homes was very clear and intrusive. They were Colombians and new to our neighborhood. They really didn't know anyone but me. She had a daughter around my age, Evelyn. I was 13 going on 14. So, Selma or Mrs. Garcia called me every afternoon around 3 PM. She invited me for a cup of coffee and sweet bakes. It was customary in her culture, and we sat in her living room. She would tell me funny stories about her country, show me photo albums of her family, and talk about anything. I was there for the food and to see Evelyn who was enchanted to be my friend. I felt the same way, too.

Selma did not have any friends yet and seemed lonely because her husband, early 50s, a short, stocky, hairy and balding man, was always working and seemed demanding. They, besides Evelyn, also had toddlers, a couple of little girls ages two and four. I always thought Evelyn was her daughter and not Mr. Garcia's because of the parents' age difference, but I kept my thoughts to myself. The little ones were very cute, and I remember they were crying most of the time because the tropical weather can be suffocating at times. They were born in Bogota where Selma claimed the weather was always desirable. Thank God she only called me when she had them sleep during siesta when she took a break. Evelyn, Mrs. Garcia, and I had these daily moments during the week to talk about anything related to any interesting narrative, books or plain small town tales. We had story-telling in common and enjoyed our moments together. Evelyn didn't say much, but she was a great audience; she liked to listen and ask questions.

The day after my previous night's vision, I was about to go back home and noticed that her rented house had not been remodeled when I looked up at her unsafe bathroom windows. I had visited them countless times but because of my paranormal vision the night before I felt compelled to talk to her about their safety. The landlord of that house seemed never interested in having any expenses invested to safeguard their property, probably to pocket as much money as he could to the detriment of the innocent tenants.

As I walked out, I backed up a few steps and said to her, "By the way, you know what, Mrs. Garcia?"

Selma turned her face to me.

"I had a dream last night," I said without sounding creepy.

I tried hard not to sound too serious about giving her any details that she wouldn't understand. Most probably I thought she would kick me out of her home thinking I was some weirdo. Yet, she seemed interested in hearing all about my dream.

"What was it about, my dear?"

I said hesitantly, "I dreamed that someone broke into your home through those right there..." I pointed towards the small vent holes, each the size of a concrete block in the bathroom.

She freaked out, went around inside the house, and quickly checked it out.

Then, she returned to the backyard patio and said, "Oh my goodness, don't say that child."

I felt really bad for making her feel that way, but I had no other way to say it. I knew her house was going to be broken into that night.

"Can you help me?" she asked as she dragged a small ladder and leaned it up against a wall to hold it in place.

She also asked me to help her measure the openings with a tape measure. We both concluded that it was impossible for any human being to fit through those vents when she commanded Evelyn to climb up and try to fit through the holes, but it seemed impossible for our untrained eyes.

"Don't worry about that," I said trying to sound confident. "It was only a dream. Don't pay any attention to me!"

Mrs. Garcia was concerned regardless. I could see it in her face. It would bother her until her husband had a talk with the house owner and have him remodel their bathroom's vents. I felt bad that I caused such trouble.

I kept repeating to myself, "I should have kept my big fat mouth shut."

That same night, around 2 AM, Selma went to her bathroom half-asleep. She never did turn the light on. She shared this later with me. She told me that all of a sudden she remembered what I had said to her earlier about the safety of her bathroom. So, she decided to look up and to her surprise saw a dark figure of a man hanging from the vents from his waist up. She didn't know what to make of it. The first thing that came to her mind was that a demon or ghost was scaring her, and she screamed so loud that the whole block around our neighborhood woke up.

Back in those days if something like that ever happened, all the neighbors came out with baseball bats, sticks and brooms, even machetes to help any neighbor in trouble. As my bedroom windows oversaw the Garcia's backyard, all I had to do was to stand in my bed to get the best view of her house. I laughed so hard every time I remember that episode. Imagine this happening at 2 AM in a country like Nicaragua. So funny indeed.

The midnight intruder was a well-known amateur crook from Selma's block. His real name was Otto Bermudez, better known as **Lagarto Juancho** (it translates to Johnnie Alligator but truly meant that the guy was a greedy dude). He was a noodle-skinny kid, probably a couple of years older than me. That night he got stuck in the vents and hung by his hips when Selma screamed like crazy. Juancho was very frightened especially because she was hitting him in the face with her old slipper. Her human reaction was to defend her life and her family if she could. That night, Mrs. Garcia had turned into a heroine, more like the Latino version of Wonder Woman.

The next day the Garcia's break-in was the joke around the whole block. The intruder was also known as the underpants crook. He used to steal people's underwear (especially those of women) around the neighborhood from our backyard clotheslines.

My intuition prevented the crime, although I was not sure where or when that incident was going to take place.

That night Juancho went further trying to break into someone's home while people were asleep, risking that someone might have a gun and kill the dumb crook. He was never confronted by anyone for his crimes because he never was caught. People could only assume it was him for the description of his victims. Also, the lights in the backyards weren't bright enough.

He ran like a deer avoiding hunters after someone fired a gunshot. He was too sleek and always escaped before anyone could lay a hand on him. Many years went by. Last I heard of *Lagarto Juancho* was that he moved to the USA and continued with his life of small crimes, selling pot and what not until one day he got caught, served jail time, and got deported back to Nicaragua in his old age. He did nothing in his life. Now he sells newspapers out on the streets around the city.

***

Years later, I realized that my gift was clairvoyance, the psychic ability to see visions of the future. The classic image of the Third Eye placed at the beginning of this story symbolizes this gift. I've struggled with this gift all my life because it has shown me so many haunted premonitions many of which are shown in this book. It is both a gift and a curse at the same time and comes with great responsibility. However, I have helped many along the way with this gift.

6.

The Death of the Innocents

"The war against evil had started,
and there was no going back."

The night before the tragedy of 9/11 in New York City was totally disturbing to me. I was living in Miami, Florida at the time, and I went to sleep without any strange incidents. The next morning, I literally woke up in a dream walking in a city with skyscrapers not really knowing my whereabouts at that particular moment and time.

I was walking near a park and wondering, "What am I doing here? Where am I? Am I dreaming? This is so real!"

I knew that I could've been in Central Park in New York. I had travelled over there once before. It was so long ago that many other cities reminded me of New York as well for their skyscrapers and the great amount of people moving in all directions.

I remember that I reached for my wallet, backpack, or for my passport without any luck. I was really confused. Then, this feeling of insecurity invaded my thoughts, and I began looking for clues. Everything seemed too fantastic to be real, or so incredible at the same time. I also had a gut feeling that there was something fishy about the whole thing. I decided to look in detail for clues to help me realize that it wasn't a dream but a premonition of a future event. Then, I noticed a small hill with green pastures and some weeds coming out of the trimmed grass.

The event was slowly unfolding before my eyes, and as I was moving along, my eyes were very observant. Suddenly, I saw these guys that looked and sounded "foreign." I heard them talk among themselves, and I couldn't make out their language or faces. They had black-hooded sweatshirts partially covering their faces. The only thing I remember seeing clearly was their dark eyes. Each man had a "machete" in his hand, which they used to cut the weeds off the green grass on the steep hill. These strange guys were all together, at least six or seven of them. They began swinging their machetes as if in an orchestrated dance. They had a watch that made a loud, tick-tock, echoing sound as they came down the hill.

For some reason, I stood there facing them and was amazed about the synchronization of their movements. They were advancing faster and faster towards me. Then I made the wrong comment to them.

"What a primitive method you people are using to mow the lawn. Just as third world countries do. How stupid is that in such a vast area?"

I was non-stop talking trash.

Next thing I knew, their machetes morphed into shotguns just like magic, and they were coming down the hill shooting at innocent bystanders.

I ran like hell. I couldn't breathe anymore, but still got away from their reach.

I arrived at this old part of town with a lot of vintage buildings with small shops and saw two women sitting in a booth having coffee and toast. They seemed to be having a pleasant conversation. They were unaware of what was going on outside the restaurant.

I thought to myself, "Hey I know them. Their faces look very familiar to me!"

I got closer, very slowly.

"Oh God, thank you," I said.

They turned around to see me, and they were my sister Marina, who lives in California, and my co-worker Jenny from my actual job back then in an upscale five-star hotel in Bal Harbor, FL. Jenny was the only person that I could associate with New York because I knew she was a native from that state. So, I went on and explained to them what had happened with those attackers out there.

My sister and Jenny seemed concerned, but not as scared and frightened as I was telling them the story. I felt my heart in my throat as I explained myself.

Jenny said to me; "Don't worry, man, nothing is gonna happen to you!" as she reached into her purse and gave me a key to her apartment.

The key was one of those skeleton keys from the time my grandmother was young. Although that key was bright and shiny, I had never seen one like that before. She gave me directions about how to get to her place until they figured something out. At that moment my head was spinning.

I began to think, "How in the world do they know each other?"

Yet, all I wanted was to be safe and get away from that area as fast as I could, so I didn't give it another thought and walked steadfastly following the directions Jenny had scribbled down on a piece of paper for me.

My mind started thinking about how Jenny was so detailed oriented in connection with the whole thing and how carefully she drew a map to go around unnoticed for a few blocks without being caught by these mad men. She also said that I could hide in her place while everything calmed down, and the word "bridge" stuck in my head.

"My apartment is the first building on the other side of the bridge on the first floor. You can't miss it!"

She said it firmly staring at me with her deep blue eyes and her Swedish looks. Anyhow, I followed her directions to the T and went to that old building on the other side of a river with green waters. I had this intuition that I've been there before, but I wasn't sure. Later, when I was crossing the bridge, there were other people walking nearby, but I remained very secretive. I did not want anyone to notice me. I was on a mission, safeguarding my valuable life.

Carefully, I reviewed the drawings on the piece of paper and noticed something odd in the distance, something strange down there moving nearby the waters.

"Oh, my goodness!"

They were a couple of very young kids who looked like identical twins, except for their height. One seemed a bit taller than the other, although both wore beautiful sailor attire like the ones my brothers and I used to wear back in the 1960s to go to church on Sundays. The kids had curly blond hair and their faces resembled famous cherubs of Renaissance art. The colors on their uniforms were those of the US Flag, red, white, and blue. The boys were walking like zombies into the river without any expressions on their faces.

I started screaming my head off to people down there.

"Help them, please, anyone help them!"

I was too high up on top of the bridge to do anything myself and way too far to even be heard by any of the bystanders near them. People were going about their own businesses. No one stopped to look. I was the only one to see their death straight in the face, and I was alone.

The twins continued their journey of walking right into the green soiled waters and unstoppably meet their end.

That wasn't all. To make things even worse, a humongous "longhorn bull" followed behind them. It slowly walked into the waters in between the twins separating the beautiful children, one to each side of the bull's head.

As I was more desperate to do something about it, I heard this firm voice with the force of many bolts of lightning coming down from the sky that clearly said:

"THE DEATH OF THE INNOCENTS"

Then, I looked back down and the child to my left had been pierced by the bull's magnificent horn on the side of his beautiful face, cutting through his skull like a knife through butter and killing him immediately.

A few minutes later, as I am crying about such a tragedy, I saw the other imposing horn transgress the other boy's face killing him. Both of the kids' eyes were open and lifeless just like stinky, dead fish. Slowly, they began to slip away, and their blood filled the green waters of the river.

All of it was over, and everything remained still for a moment. I was there alone again when all kinds of debris and ashes came down from the sky snowing all over the city and the riverbank. I couldn't help but inconsolably cry over their deaths because I saw what happened ahead of time, but I couldn't do a damn thing about it.

I yelled to the skies above, "Why me?"

***

Later at Jenny's apartment, after all that drama and commotion, my phone was ringing off the hook and awakened me. I jumped out of bed and grabbed it.

"Hellooo!" my sister Marina from California called.

She was crying and sounded very distressed and very loud!

"What's up, sis? What's going on?!" I said in Spanish.

"Turn your TV on right now and see the news!"

I did immediately, and it was at the moment when the scene of the first attack on the tower of the World Trade Center was being replayed. They were talking about it as if it was an accident. Suddenly, to my surprise a second plane crashed live on TV at the same moment they declared a possible act of terrorism was unfolding in our nation. I was in shock and hung up the phone on my sister, who I also imagined was in shock.

My mind slowly reacted to the moment of truth where I realized I was let in on the horrible tragedy where the war against evil had started, and there was no going back.

***

In hindsight, I realized that I had received a clairvoyant vision of this tragedy. The symbolism of the masked gardeners dressed in black with machetes were the terrorists with box cutters. The twin boys were the twin towers and the bull's horns slicing into them were the alleged planes crashing into the buildings. I was only a witness to the whole thing. The truth is that I know I ran off scared by their

71

actions, but I instinctively knew that regardless of these fears those evil dudes were in another dimension.

In the end, my mind rushed with many crazy thoughts, and the real intention was for me to run to a specific spot (the twin towers) where all this tragedy was taking place in real time. Even though I had this clairvoyant vision (my paranormal gift!), I knew there was nothing I could do. I was shown the truth and reality of how things work here on Earth. I know in the future I'll be some sort of a jury participant, and that's why I was let in on this secret knowledge. That is my job. I can't stop anything. I am only a little being in this world. I know that we all have the power to change the world and its evil ways, but we need to change from within one by one to make that change.

7.

The Ancient Columns

"I saw the huge illuminating craft
come down by the edge of the landscape
near the ancient columns."

How do I explain how I got here, who took me, why was I taken, and when was I taken?

All I can remember was that I traveled in a strange cocoon made of a hard, resistant material, yet a manageable gel of some sort, and I was able to breath oxygen. Going back to the beginning of this experience, before all this happened to me, I felt a powerful wind blowing through. The speed can only be compared to jumping out of an airplane without a parachute. I wished I had goggles over my eyes because I felt tears running unstoppably down my cheeks as the wind was putting pressure on them and on my skin. The cocoon was more like a transparent body bag or a body mold to keep my body still. I also had another feeling: the sensation of being in this gel when I was moving my arms and legs if I wanted to. I hit maximum speed which finally came to a sudden halt, as I slowed down in a fraction of a second. Regardless of how weird all that was, I did enjoy the trip and felt safe and without any fear.

I was on another planet like Earth. Yet, it was sort of an artificial moon with atmosphere. There was no sun, but it was illuminated on its own. Far out in the distance, I saw a vast and beautiful landscape with such greatness to it and without any trees, rocks, or any imaginable natural resource that I could relate to on Earth, as I knew it. I was given this temporary knowledge about being a guest to a lecture, an event of great importance. The place was right there, where I landed (no idea but it didn't resemble my world). I was there in flesh and blood. The area where the ancient structure was had a corridor and a huge plaza in its surroundings. I was very observant of it all even though I was quite a distance away. The ancient structure resembled a Roman or Greek temple sustained by many sets of columns. I was not totally sure why I was there. Still, it was as if I had been expecting this event throughout my life.

The structures had brilliance to them as if they were kept clean forever and as if they were built only with the finest marble I had ever seen. The columns had golden tones, and they really had illumination of their own. Even the roads seemed to have been made of pure silver gold.

Then "*bang*!" It hit me!

I was a part of a huge crowd of men with white beards on their chins. Most had silver hair as if they were all in their 60s. There were thousands of them, and they all looked older than me as if they came from different times and eras in human history. I was with them. I was a part of this awesome crowd. I was standing there next to them and wondering many things. I was very vigilant of all things. The ground under our feet was made of the greatest quality of silver, and the stones were created or crafted in pure gold. Natural or not, they seemed to fit specifically with the scenery. There was no green grass or signs of any type of weed or Earth soil anywhere. Everyone, including me, was barefoot and had white tunics on that seemed to be made of the finest cotton. The place also seemed to me that it was used only for certain events just like the one I'm writing about now.

I ran my hands through the tunic. It was so comfortable and felt as if it was a mix of wool and cotton.

I thought to myself, "I hate wool!"

Yet, the one I had on felt like the most comfortable piece of garment I had ever worn in my entire life. It felt so good on my body.

Everyone there, just like me, was expecting something. I didn't know what, but I suspected it. I tried to keep myself in a low profile since I felt like a fly on a glass of milk. When suddenly as I looked at everyone's faces, they seemed to know what was going to happen in the next minute or so. Meanwhile, I felt displeased with the fact that I could've been there by mistake. I had no idea whatsoever and worried that I could be ejected from that place in front of the whole crowd. For a moment, I felt like an outcast who didn't belong there.

Lots of vehicles made of glass and all sorts of other crafts flew over "the sky," if you can call it that. They all were illuminated, twinkled like stars, and moved like insects do in the woods.

Each one of them was in a group. More men landed in these fields, and their craft movements were so silent. Each landed as if they posed like flies soundlessly on the area assigned to them. The men who came down from these objects walked very solemnly and calmly to fill their spots on the plaza. My eyes moved from one place to another as if I wanted to cover all bases. I wanted to remember every single detail, although there was so much I couldn't keep from thinking that they would last me a lifetime.

Then, a voice came down from the sky and announced, "The speaker has arrived."

At this moment, I started trembling and sweating cold and hot at the same time. I could feel the sticky sweat all over my body and forehead. I couldn't help but feel very uneasy. My mind was racing with a thousand thoughts. My jaw started to shiver uncontrollably. I was in so much fear.

Everyone there kept an eye on the center of the plaza where this huge and fantastic craft made of glass, shooting bright lights from within, landed on the main field. There was no way anyone could have missed that great landing. It was so majestic at the same time.

My simple human words can't describe what I got to see with my very own eyes. At that moment everyone bowed down to their knees. I have to admit I was so frightened when I saw the huge, illuminating craft come down by the edge of the landscape near the ancient columns. As much as I wanted to be a part of the crowd and just walk amongst them, I couldn't bend my knees, and as much as I tried to fall on my rear, I just couldn't get myself to do just that. I was worried and frightened because of it. I felt as if I was being a rebel myself.

A voice came from above with the sound of ten thousand harps:

"THE ANTICHRIST"

The commotion on the crowd was unbearable. I heard their cries and their screaming as they ran in all directions. I stood there watching the whole entanglement, and nothing reached me because I was on top of a nearby hill. I couldn't believe my crying eyes and ears for such a great tragedy. Then, everything turned black and void, and darkness conquered the light, and I wasn't there any longer.

***

Looking back, I was summoned to be a witness of future events in humanity, in this case, a big deception and worldwide religious event. Once a human dies, or isn't born yet, they are in a state of total wisdom and all knowledge. It's very hard for them to be confused or lost, yet in that realm the biggest secret is that there's a way for a spiritual deception regardless and that is how the battle in the sky was lost once before.

I was there the same way we travel in real time by our most advance technology. It wasn't on Earth; it was in a world that isn't a place for living but for meetings and gatherings. It's a physical world light years away in a hidden dimension of the universe in between the twin stars of the northern constellations from Earth where only the most advanced type of humans could gather. It is not just for any human unless they're a part of that specifically developed race.

8.

The Ghost in Nona's House

"She was the same ghost I remember from my nightmare."

Ever since my early childhood, my sixth sense tapped into other dimensions. I was showered with amazing abilities. Sometimes I was afraid but other times, it let me see into a dimension not allowed to be known to most people. That walk into the unknown was something I preserved in a special place in my "memory bank" as those mysteries that I've witnessed unwillingly evolved in my mind to become a part of who I am and what it is I needed to do in this life. Back in the late 1960s when I was around seven years old, I came to experience a series of events during my childhood and paid a high price just for being who I was.

There was a nice lady in my neighborhood who was dearly named Nona Duarte. She lived just a few houses away from my home. Nona was surrounded by an evil presence that tried to make contact with me from beyond the grave. The most I remember about her was that she was an elderly and sickly woman in her early 60s. She kept to herself and almost never came out to socialize at any events like other neighbors did. Señora Nona's home had a very large backyard with a few fruit trees always in full bloom with juicy fruits guarded by a five-foot red brick fence that kept most kids my age away, except me, and some of my friends. We had gained Nona's trust perhaps because my parents were close to her family.

She was all smiles to us. The only rule she asked of us was to make sure that we didn't shake or break the branches of the trees. She also requested to not take the fruits that were not fully ripe. She had a big stick to pluck the fruits with, so we nicely asked her if we could use it. Once we had enough of the fruits, we took off. Sometimes, we forgot to ask for permission because she never said anything to us anyway, as kids will be kids. Nona always looked at us at an angle behind the curtains of her windows not really in a creepy way, but more like a mother. She never complained about us being there more often than we should have, so we played fools and kept helping ourselves to some more fruits. It was like heaven to us.

Nona and her husband had grown about five different tropical fruit trees in their backyard. I loved guava and *Jocotes* (Nicaraguan plums) but MANGOES were our favorite ones. We loved to prepare green, half-ripe mangoes. We would peel them off, slice them, put salt, dark vinegar and a little bit of Tabasco sauce in the mix, and voila, we had a heavenly sin. It was a delicacy for us kids back in those days. We liked anything tangy, sour, and salty, and since Nona never said or complained about our presence there, we made it a habit to be there like flies around her backyard.

She seemed like a lonely housewife who dedicated her life to her neatly dressed husband. I remember some elderly and nosy neighbor, Mrs. Reyes (rest her soul), said that the Duartes had a beautiful daughter named Lita (nickname for Adelita). I'd never heard of her until that very day, but rumors had it that she married an old gringo from New York City, and they moved away to live their lives away from her family. Lita never returned to Nicaragua. The main reason she left was because of a psychopathic "ex-fiancée" she had in the military. He was an abusive ape that used to beat her up when she was still so much younger than him. Mrs. Reyes, the self-motivated, neighborhood tongue lash, continued delighting the nosy women who gathered around her to hear the juicy gossip. She went on saying that Lita was afraid her ex would do harm to her or her family, so she'd rather marry a foreigner and walk away from her awful past. Early in life, I've learned that to some people someone else's life was more appealing than their own.

Mr. Duarte was a man in his early 40s, well-dressed and well taken care by his elderly wife. He used to travel to the USA once a year to visit his daughter but without Nona, his wife, perhaps because she was always sick. Who knows? When I heard that story, I felt bad for Señora Nona's daughter. I felt that her daughter should have come and visited her instead, but it was not my business. I just thought so because I always have an opinion. Mr. Duarte was an executive who worked for a German corporation. I believe it had to do with typewriters or something related to that field. He owned a very small Italian car; he was a salesman and a technician at the same time. Most people had a monster car made of heavy steel, like my dad's car. We used to call it "The Green Hornet," although the car was black.

I liked Mr. Duarte's style. For an older man, I thought he was some kind of a playboy regardless of his age. He was very well spoken, and his wife kept his tidy image to the extreme. Some old, nosy housewives claimed they had seen Nona kneeling down, taking his shoes off and putting his slippers on as if she were a *Japanese Geisha*. They'd complain that no woman should be their husband's slave. I knew most of them were housewives and that some of their husbands kept them on a very short leash. Yet, they loved to unleash their tongues to feed their hunger for evil, secretive talk.

Mr. Duarte was friends with my dad. Sometimes they went on a guy's night out and indulged in the bars around the city of Managua with another bunch of guys from their school and childhood years. Dad always maintained that his buddy, Mr. Duarte, was the life of the party. In my head I felt sorry for Nona and wondered why the women in the neighborhood would not have a ladies' night out the same way the guys did. Back in those years women's liberties were limited. Just to continue with their career goals and work was enough freedom for them per our backwards society. At my young age, I already knew that was totally unfair. My mom was the exception among other women her age. She broke all the rules and molds in her own time. Mom did all those things and more. My dad was not a ridiculous kind of man full of himself, thank God.

Mr. Duarte usually came to our home to seek father's professional advice. Dad was a very successful businessman, and many friends would come to do just that. My dad was cool about it, and he would take his own time to share a few of his successful tips. Although very seldom, my dad visited their homes unless they had a party where drinking and mariachis were involved. Mr. Duarte would show up without his wife. He was a kind man, very playful with my siblings and me. He always had a handful of mint candies in his hands and told my sister to split it among all of us. My mom felt Nona being all alone in her empty home was not a good idea because she suffered from depression. Once in a while, we went to see her. I was the youngest in the house, so she took me everywhere. I told my mom I started to feel like a monkey on a leash because I often wasn't so pleased to go. Mom got a kick out of my antics with a funny smirk on her face.

When we visited Nona, I was impressed at the way her home looked. She kept it very clean and without a maid. It was her little palace she'd say with a strange, sick cough. Everything was so well kept and shiny that I marveled to see such cleanliness in her home, but of course, she did not have any large pets or kids around the house.

She only had a green parrot named **Toñita**. The parrot was polite and spoke clearly just like a real human. **Toñita** always greeted people and said things like, "Pepe is cute," "Pepe is nice," and, "I love Pepe." She also said, "Welcome to Pepe's home," and I was truly impressed every time. When it was about time for us to leave, she would say a very formal goodbye, "Thank you for visiting Pepe's home. We'll see ya next time you decide to drop by." Pepe belonged to Mr. Duarte. I think that Mrs. Duarte probably had the funny bird trained for months to sound as clear as that.

I got the feeling that those phrases the bird implied every time were very significant, and I had a bad feeling instead of being amazed at my age. I probably did not understand many things, but that was my intuition because I could read between the lines. I felt that Nona was going to crash and burn in her relationship. My parents thought it was cute and made no comments about it. I had my reservations and kept my opinion to myself. Back in those days, the word divorce was taboo in my country.

On my way back from school one day, it was drizzling and that was no fun. What that meant was no playing in the park for the kids that day. As I was going home quickly to avoid getting wet, I noticed Nona getting into her husband's car. I greeted her.

She said, "See ya later, kiddo. I'm going to the doctor," pointing at me to keep an eye on her house.

I smiled and nodded as I kept rushing towards my home. It was a bit after noon. Then, about an hour later, the weather conditions drastically changed to a beautiful sunny day with blue skies. I did what other kids from around the block did; I went to play in the park. Later on, the bad weather returned again, amazingly, a bit stronger than before. Incredibly, it turned into a heavy rain, the kind that felt like airsoft gun bullets on the skin. It darkened the whole city at around 3 PM, I recall. So, my friends and I ran to hide under the big trees to avoid most of the cold rain, yet it was difficult to keep dry since the wind was blowing the branches and leaves away. No matter what we tried, in the end we got soaking wet. Eventually, everyone took off to their own homes running and yelling like crazies, "See you fools!" I was afraid I could be hit by lightning. I've read in the newspaper about people doing the same and a bolt of lightning killed them. That scared me out of my wits.

Lolo was a boy who always hung out in my gang. I remember that both of us ran in the same direction. We were jumping in every pool of mud that we found on the way even if we tried our best to avoid them. Lolo lived just a few houses before the Duartes' home, and I remembered that Mr. and Mrs. Duarte weren't home. That meant we had the whole backyard to ourselves without being watched by Nona's inquisitive looks!

"Let's go to the Duartes and get some mangoes!" I yelled under the heavy rain.

To my surprise, the boy declined. He claimed that he didn't feel that well and wanted to go home to change his wet clothes. So, I walked by Nona's home, climbed the redbrick fence and saw those plums and juicy mangoes waiting for any kind soul to pluck them and take them away from those branches. To my amazement, some on the very top of the trees were ripe. I walked slowly and looked around the backyard. The windows were closed, and the house seemed deserted.

I thought to myself, "I will get in and grab as many mangoes as I could. I have no competition today!"

I took off my t-shirt and made a knot at the end of it to make it into a temporary sack. I started plucking all the fruits that I could carry. On the top of my favorite tree, I saw the juiciest mango that I had ever seen in my entire life.

"Oh no! How can I reach it? It's so high up!" I thought when I tried to turn my head to look all the way up the treetop. I wouldn't forgive myself if that mango didn't leave the premises without me.

I acted out of impulse without thinking of the consequences of my actions. I took my shoes off and climbed the tree as fast as I could. I was feeling fully motivated by the size of that humongous mango. Once up there, I was very close to grabbing the juicy light green and reddish mango when I had the sensation that someone was looking at me with piercing eyes. It made me turn my face towards a window in the Duartes' master bedroom and see a reflection like a flash of light. I could barely see a pair of yellowish eyes from behind a curtain that jerked a bit. I felt the presence of evil inside the house. Next, lightning with the power of a hand grenade struck a nearby power line pole.

The mango tree started to tremble. I was still up there. All of this happened at the same time and caused me to lose my balance and fall to the ground. It was as high as five meters down onto the ground. I had a serious laugh attack, and then a ferocious barking got me on my feet in one quick jump. It sounded like a couple of mad dogs surrounded me. I tried to run but I was a little confused from the fall. I started to yell for help and scream. I was totally frightened by the whole situation. The funny thing was that I didn't see the beasts, yet I felt them very close to me. I felt their fur and breathing, so I started to run like hell leaving all the mangoes and my personal stuff behind. I was shaking like a leaf and very terrified.

The only thing I remember at that frightening moment was that I needed to jump the fence, but as much as I tried, I failed in every attempt to climb that fence because I couldn't let go of my shoes in one of my hands. The damn annoying dog barks weren't helping either. That's funny, but I never got to see those dogs I heard barking. Now that I think about it, Señora Nona had no dogs.

Many thoughts rushed through my head, and finally some help arrived. I could hear people on the other side of the fence. They were a couple of boys from the neighborhood, Mateo and Jean, who heard my loud desperation. They carefully jumped on top of the red brick fence to see what was going on since I was screaming like a wounded beast. Oh God! When I saw those two, I clung to their arms like my life depended on it but dropping one shoe back inside the Duartes' property. The boys helped me to get out of that darn trap.

When I was finally out, I ran like hell without explaining anything to them. I suppose they did not understand my actions. I ran home fast and then went around to the back of my house, so I did not have to explain myself to anyone who saw the frightened look on my face. Thank God, my folks were still at work. I dried myself with a towel, went straight to my room, and locked myself in. I slept for almost an hour. I remember I was still shaking with fear, not only for the experience itself but because the rain was unusually colder than ever.

The rain stopped again, and I woke up. As I was moving around in my bed, I heard three knocks at the main door of the house.

Our maid shouted, "One moment, please!"

I heard someone utter something that I could not hear well enough. I couldn't guess if it was a male or a female voice from my bedroom. I was a little far from the main door and the double French doors to my bedroom were shut, but I heard something about a package. All I remember was that I heard my name loud and clear. The maid probably thought I was asleep. I was curious and got out of the room. I opened the door slowly and walked towards the package. I remember I was expecting a parcel in the mail, a magic set I had my mom order for me. A few weeks ago, I had my birthday and requested that my mom purchase through a mail catalog a magician set (Fu Manchu). It was an original set of magic tricks with a real magician hat and a rabbit (so they claimed). I did not know what to expect and was wondering if the rabbit was alive inside a sealed package or if he was able to breathe.

I was so excited when I peeked into the package thinking about my new toy, but to my disappointment, what I found was all the stuff I had left behind at the Duartes: my t-shirt, a single shoe, and the mangoes neatly placed inside.

"What the heck? How was that possible?" I thought.

Everything I left behind was now in great shape. The shoe was clean and dry, and my t-shirt was folded and smelled clean and fresh. The mangoes had the skin washed and were bright and ready to sink my teeth into.

All I wondered was, "How can it be?"

I knew for a fact that Nona didn't have a washing machine, nor have I ever seen one that could do that kind of work in so little time.

"A sophisticated machine that could do all that kind of stuff in a matter of minutes? Nah!"

I'd always see Nona washing clothes by hand in her backyard. There was no sunshine peeking over the sky, yet to even think that Nona had dried everything under the sun was unbelievable to me. It was still dark out and drizzling still. So, I went up to Mina, our maid, and asked her about the package.

She replied, "Some lady."

I tried again in disbelief, "Mrs. Duarte?"

She looked at me with that lost look typical of her, "No, it was some woman I never seen around!"

"Some woman, she'd never seen? How strange!" I thought to myself.

I was left in the dark again. I couldn't explain any of it in my head either.

I grabbed the juicy mango and ate it without giving it another thought. After that, I went back to lie down in my bed and dreamed that I was back on Nona's patio. Everything repeated itself in this foggy dream of mine, although this time the events materialized little by little in my dream. I saw a couple of mad dogs chasing me to sink their sharp teeth into my bare legs. Then, a spirit of a woman rose up from a wet puddle filled with mud. The strange woman had a white, dirty gown and a set of horrible, yellowish, reflecting eyes that looked like feline eyes. The ghost or spirit came closer to me and spoke to my face. A cloudy mist surrounded her. The woman floated in midair, her legs hung loose, but she had no feet. Her arms were like a rag doll, also hanging to the sides. She had Native American hair, black, straight and long to her waist line.

She said right in my face, "Welcome to Pepe's home."

I tried to yell out loud, but I was paralyzed—first the dogs, and now a spirit. I tried to run the heck out of there but couldn't. She then turned up into the air. There was some lightning, and she came back again.

"Thank you for visiting Pepe's home," she said.

There was another lightning strike as she floated around and disappeared through the window that overlooked the patio. I was released from these invisible, strong hands and ran the heck out as fast as I could. When I was running my feet sank into the mud. Some hands came out of the mud and grabbed my feet. As I was screaming, I woke up in a cold sweat. I remember that I prayed to my guardian angel and felt at peace after that.

***

Years went by and I never set foot in Nona's house again because of that traumatizing incident. My own friends wanted me to go back with them to the Duartes' home to pluck some mangoes off of the tree, but I declined every time. I never went back to that haunted house again. It wasn't a pretty experience to deal with that demon with the yellowish evil eyes. I never talked about it and did not want people to think I was chased by evil. I was afraid of losing their friendship or people's trust, although I couldn't do anything about the ones that already knew me. It was my own secret with the paranormal.

One day some lady told my mom that Nona was terminally ill and that her daughter Lita had come from the United States to care for her ailing mother in her final days. Mom took me along to pay Nona a visit so many years after that scary incident in her backyard. I kind of heard Nona speaking a few words and right after that she fell into a deep sleep. That evening, I finally met Adelita, her pretty daughter. She was suffering a great deal about her mother's poor health issues. Yet, she managed a sparkling smile with perfect white teeth. She explained to my mom that she came with her foreign husband, but he wasn't there when we arrived.

The Ghost in Nona's House

There were five women with my mom and Lita having a conversation about Nona's health conditions. Bartolo Garza stepped out of Nona's room; he was a man of the cloth, a Catholic priest from our local church. Father Garza was a great man with a strong personality. He was a native of Spain, "The Mother Land." His heavy Spanish accent showed when he pronounced an "s" like a "z." I tried to use it sometimes, but I bit my tongue every single time. So for "sopa de pollo," which means chicken soup, he'd pronounce it "zopa de pollo." I got a kick out of his pronunciation; I thought that it was so cute.

Other than that, he was a cool priest and very charismatic, but strict and loud. He told the ladies that he performed the last rites and that she was able to accept the holy sacrament. He said that she was already prepared to take the journey now. I felt my eyes opening wide when listening to all that weird talk. Then, he explained he had a lot of work to do at his church. Adelita was thankful with the priest and kissed his hand. He gazed at me letting me know he noticed me, so I forced a shy smile.

Father Garza had a black leather pouch he always carried around for his dying faithful. With his small hands, he pulled a leather string from the pouch, closed it, and then left the house.

I thought to myself, "Oh my, she's gone."

Every time I heard something like "last rites," people would die soon after. I thought that was scary! The women spoke in such low, sad tones. People were coming in and out of Nona's room. I wondered about that demon I saw a few years back in that very same room, the one with evil eyes hiding behind the curtains. I don't think anyone noticed me when I decided to snoop around Nona's bedroom.

Then, someone knocked at the door. It was Doctor Leguizamo. He walked into the house and acknowledged everyone presence.

"Good day, everyone!"

89

Lita knew him all right; it was their family doctor for the way their conversation was going. Actually, he was the whole neighborhood's family doctor. He was my doctor, too. He delivered me and all my siblings, and he knew every kid's name around my neighborhood. I'm sure he delivered Lita as well. She grabbed him by his arm and accompanied him into her mother's room; they took a few minutes while he checked her blood pressure, breathing, and whatever the doctors do in a delicate situation like that of Nona's. Dr. Leguizamo came out of the room first, followed by Lita who had a comely appearance. Some of the ladies asked him about her condition.

"Delicate, but stable," he said, yet his expression was sending the wrong signals.

The women kept flooding him with more questions; they wanted to hear what he had to say. This was the only chance I had to greet Nona or just say "hi" to her. She was by herself in the room. I felt drawn to her as if some mysterious energy was pulling me to go into Nona's room. I wanted to look for that presence that had something to say.

Finally, I went into Nona's room. Nona was totally sedated; she had terminal cancer, a terrible disease back when it was a death sentence and people didn't know much about it. All they could do for her was to keep her doped. I looked around and thought to myself how funny is was that she had pink veils hanging from the ceiling and other ridiculous, very feminine choices of colors. I couldn't imagine her manly husband sleeping in a princesslike room. How funny that was to me. I didn't notice the smirk I had on my face when everyone was teary-eyed. Soon, I felt my mom's look on the back of my neck as if she wanted to squeeze it. I, of course, had to put every effort into hanging the look on my face and turn it into a sad puppy dog.

I was being curious. Nona's eyes had these rapidly involuntary movements. Then, I heard a rattling noise coming from the giant closet in the room. One of the doors was slightly open, and I walked towards it in little halting steps. Suddenly, I saw those horrifying, glowing, yellow eyes again in the dark end behind the closet door, just like a freaking buzzard circling around dead animals in the wild. Without hesitation, I rushed the hell out of that room.

Next, I heard this creepy voice say, "Welcome to Pepe's home."

It was *Toñita*; she quite startled me. They had placed the parrot's cage near Señora Nona's bed in a corner; in case she opened her eyes, she could see her precious bird directly from her angle. The doctor said it was good therapy.

Nobody even noticed me acting all nervous and wanting to get the heck out. I ran towards my mother, grabbed her hand, and begged her to please let us go home, but she hushed me saying that was not polite. My heart was pounding. I felt that I couldn't breathe, and then I got the hiccups. At that point my mom was really upset, and she sent me home on my own. She felt that I was behaving like a naughty boy, and I had a few of her fulminating looks. I knew what that meant and had no choice.

Slowly, I regained my serenity and pretended it was not a big deal. I looked around peacefully. I stayed another minute. My mother ignored me and got back to her conversation with the rest of the women. A kind, elderly lady in the group named Doña Simona asked Adelita about her dad, and she said something very quietly in response like, "he's out with my husband." She went on explaining about funeral arrangements with tears on her face, and I couldn't avoid my fear of death.

A few minutes later, I heard Mr. Duarte's small car approaching the house, and the headlights peeked through the curtains. A minute or so later, the door opened and the odd couple walked in: Bobby (Lita's husband) was a tall guy and Mr. Duarte was the opposite, a very short man. I thought it was very funny and that made me forget the horrible ghostly experience I had in Nona's room at least for a minute or two. Pepe put his hand on my very short hair as usual and messed it up. I hated older men who would do that, but I forced a smile because in those days you wouldn't dare express your opinions to any adults. The North American had a funny fisherman's hat on and a ridiculous shirt with crazy flowers and bright colors he called a Hawaiian shirt. He spoke broken Spanish to me with a funny accent.

"Hey chavalo, como va?" (Hey buddy, what's up?)

I smiled and said nothing as I swung my feet on the rocking chair.

Toñita's feathers were standing on end, and she was being a little too loud for comfort in the background, yet no one cared but me. I was trembling already. I knew her wild behavior had to do with the apparition. I buggered off silently and ran like a wild hare to get home before the ghost caught up with me. I entered through the backdoor to avoid anyone.

Oh, my goodness, I found my dad as usual reading the newspaper and smoking a cigarette in the indoor patio sitting in a rocking chair. He knew I was with my mom.

He asked me, "Where's your mom?"

I mumbled something that did not make sense and kept walking. He went back to his newspaper, and I hid in my room.

Many years have passed since that silent evening, but still I remember everything very clearly in my head. I was already in bed and started to get really warm in my room. So, I turned the fan on and covered myself with the sheets. A thought about Nona got into my mind, and I felt deeply sad for her. Ooooh, who would've thought that every time I remember her weary eyes and her sweetness that it would bring tears to my eyes? I knew in my heart she would live a bit longer than what everyone expected she would, but for sure, she was not going to make it through the end of that week. It's as if I knew. I always predicted things before they happened. She was a kind woman, a saint. She was the only person in the neighborhood that did not send us away when we asked her if she would allow us to pluck fruits off her trees. One funny thing about Nona that cracked me up all these years was that she never got involved in gossip or assisted in any of the community parties, like most women did. Instead, she kept to herself. Yet, Nona knew what went around in our community.

A few days later Señora Duarte passed away. Father Garza celebrated a mass in her memory. The church was swamped with a great crowd of people, and my buddies and I were outside looking at her coffin from the church's windows. We were playing marbles. I competed for the biggest marble and won regardless of tears running down my cheeks. Nona was the nicest lady I'd ever met in my life then, and I would never get to see her again.

The next day she was buried, and no one said anything in public. They stared at her coffin and at Mr. Duarte like zombies. On that occasion before her burial, there was a walking procession and most locals were there. When people died in my country and they seemed to be quiet and not as social with everyone, I always wondered how come so many people showed up at their funeral. Nona wasn't that popular, nor had any real friends within the community. Likewise, so was her husband, who was a very quiet guy when he wasn't drunk.

Pepe, his daughter Adelita, and Bobby moved at a regular and fairly slow pace by lifting and setting down each foot in turn with the multitude towards *el Panteon del Refugio* (Haven Memorial Cemetery, our local graveyard). We walked along with the rest of the crowd. Nona's casket was placed on top of the funeral motor coach with lots of the finest flower arrangements you can imagine. It was beginning to rain; a drizzle wet everyone's heads. Men wore elegant fedora dress hats and black suits regardless of the hot weather conditions, usually year-round, classic tropical weather. When we finally arrived to *el Panteon*, we stayed back, and those without hats or raincoats ducked under a large roof. Father Garza was in the middle of the flock carrying umbrellas. The priest said a few words of consolation for their great loss. He then prayed a psalm reading from a small Bible. The priest's voice was so strong he did not need a microphone yet someone provided him with one of those horrible megaphones. We hardly understood the distorted psalm because it was way too loud.

"The Lor_ is my she_erd; I shall not _ant. He _kes me lie down in gre_ pastures. He leads me side still waters. He _stores my soul. He leads me in paths of righ_usness for his name's sake. Even though I _lk through the _alley of the shadow of death, I will _r no evil, for you are with me; your rod and your staff, they _fort me."

As the holy man finished the psalm, a lightning bolt struck at close range, and the rain got stronger. The folks with their black-and-white umbrellas rushed to hide from the mayhem. Mr. Duarte was holding on to the biggest umbrella to cover his daughter and himself from the wild storm. Pepe reminded me of the penguin in the Batman sequels on television. I couldn't help to form a funny smirk on my face, regardless of the mourning that was taking place at the moment. They were crying inconsolably. Bobby was holding Lita's hand. It was an appalling scene of sadness and sorrow. I couldn't feel any guiltier than I did that afternoon for thinking about the funny TV character.

Kids were playing around the burial grounds. I was behaving extremely well for my age. I had a great respect for the dead, so I kept to myself and ignored my friends when they called me to play with them.

An elegant lady dressed in white stood out from the crowd for her unique appearance. She seemed familiar to me but had a hat with a white veil covering her face, so I couldn't tell who she was. Yet, I kept an eye on her.

Six men close to the Duartes, including Bobby and Pepe, lifted Nona's coffin helped by the gravediggers. All of them slowly laid her in the hole helped by rope and a lot of physical strength. The grave was filled with mud and loose dirt, and I counted every shovel of soil dumped into that hole. Then all those beautiful flowers were placed on top of the dirt where Nona's cold and stiff body will remain until kingdom come. I have to admit that those who stayed by the Duartes, including my folks, were good people because they risked getting scorched by another lightning strike.

With such a multitude standing there, I couldn't get a clear picture of what went on, but I heard a loud cry and commotion. One thing I do remember very clearly that scared me was when Pepe loudly yelled to be buried with his loving wife of a lifetime. He almost fainted. Most women cried and expressed their painful emotions. I'll be darned, but nothing was so clear after that.

I got closer to the mystery lady in white. She turned her face and caught me staring. She looked like Nona's twin sister in her good years, not that I knew if she had any, but I couldn't tell as there was a lot going on. I took a few steps back to have a better look. I freaked out and took my eyes off her when a sudden breath of wind forced me to lose my balance. An unsuspected hand helped me to stay put. I turned and there she was, the lady in white.

"Oh gee!" I thought.

She was the same ghost I remember from my nightmare.

"Oh, my goodness!" She was real!

She opened her mouth and blasted me with a vile stupor, "Get out of here!"

She scared the wits out of me. I took a step back and fell on my butt. I tried to get up, remembering her on many occasions hanging around Nona all of this time.

"How could I forget those reflecting, yellowish eyes? They were evil!"

I tried to scream, but she appeared to have vanished into thin air. I thought to myself that it probably was my imagination that was really crazy. One way or the other, I was truly frightened by whatever that was.

No one around me seemed to be affected by it. Yet a girl who was nearby named Juana asked me if I was okay. I nodded "yes" but kept to myself. Juana had come with other kids, the ones playing by the graves as soon as the rain got stronger.

Nona had died on a Friday night and was buried the next day probably around 1 PM. I left with everyone else. This time I did not run; I was tired of running even from death.

That night, the music was so loud in the "party zone" just a couple of blocks away from our neighborhood. Live mariachis were playing happy and romantic songs. All the action was inside the local bars and on the sidewalks, a place full of tables filled with drunk men and women.

We were coming home from a soccer game. I felt as if I had eaten something that got me bloated. We always had fun watching the drunk people dancing, telling their funny jokes, or enjoying their time together like when my dad was drunk with his friends. Although after Nona's funeral, we weren't so cheerful, and no one had any humor to hang around this time.

Then Lolo said, "Hey, check it out. Mr. Duarte is dancing with a nice lady."

"WHAT?!" I said. I was in shock. "How in the world would he be doing that when his wife was just buried today?"

I went closer to see it with my own eyes. There he was dancing his life away, drunk like hell and being loud celebrating life. I thought he did not drink or smoke, but it seemed like those were imprudent comments about his unimpeachable image. However, what I saw in that bar (The Sea of Tranquility) that evening was not Mr. Duarte but a wild crazy and unknown man. He was acting like a real devil with horns and tail, but then again, he was probably disturbed for his loss and that behavior was helping him to cope with his grief.

"Who knows?!" I thought.

A couple of old hags walking by also saw him having the time of his life. The women used their hands to cross their faces and bodies as if they had encountered evil.

One of them said, "What a shame that his wife was buried today, and he has already forgotten about that!"

I took off and went home very disappointed with humanity.

That night, I dreamed that I was at Nona's home, grabbing some mangoes. She walked in a white gown with a veil just like I saw the ghost in the cemetery that afternoon. She caught us on her property. It was a weird kind of encounter without a word said. She was carrying something in her hands: *Toñita*, the green parrot. It looked stiff and very dead to me, and then I realized that it was her spirit wandering about.

She floated above the ground, and then she said in an eerie voice, "Welcome to Pepe's home."

"Wow!"

It was Nona herself who said it; she had tears running down her face. The parrot turned white and flew away, and Nona vanished into thin air just like the ghost at the cemetery.

I looked towards the window and saw the yellowish evil eyes again. I abruptly woke up breathing heavily. I was exhausted. I couldn't keep up with the evil spirit still lingering in my memory and dreams. I thanked God that I heard my folks coming home. I felt safe again, and I could sleep without any further incidents.

A week later, Adelita Duarte-O'Bryan returned to the USA with her husband Bobby. As soon as they left the very next day, Mr. Duarte brought a mistress named Lencha into his home that became "The Scandal of the Year" amongst the neighbors. People said many things, but Pepe told Mrs.

Reyes that he didn't give a rat's ass what anyone had to say about him. He sacrificed a lot for his wife, and now she rests in peace until kingdom come.

***

In hindsight, I do not have any explanation for the ghost in Nona's house. I do know that the house was built over ancient Mayan sacrificial grounds and that may have had something to do with it. In my home, just a few houses away from Nona's, we had the presence of ghostly witches and old hags, which only my mom and I had the ability to see into the dimensions. The history of our house was that an innocent woman was raped, murdered, and hung by a tree on our property. I can only speculate that the ghost of the woman who was hung attracted the other ghosts that were often seen in our house.

By the same reasoning, I can only guess that a similar traumatized death was the reason for the ghost's appearance in Nona's house and that I was the only one who could see her. No one else would believe me, not even my mom. No doubt part of the problem was that I was so young and thought to be filled with a wild imagination. Although the ghost terrified me, she also showed me a strange compassion by manifesting in human form long enough to deliver a package containing my missing shoe, t-shirt, and mangoes, all mysteriously clean.

Later in life, I learned that when a human undergoes a traumatic death, often a ghost appears afterwards and is thought by some to be a lonely soul that has lost all knowledge about returning to the etheric realm for healing. So, the ghost wanders this third dimensional plane seeking answers from the living. Unfortunately, that often results in feeding off the negative energy of fear from those who are afraid of them, leading the ghost to remain trapped on this plane indefinitely.

Other times, it can result in the ghost getting sympathetic directions from an aware human that it must return to the etheric realm. The ghost can sometimes be escorted there by angels if called upon by the human assisting them.

I must confess that I was too young to understand this way of helping lost souls back then and was, therefore, always scared to death of them because of their otherworldly presence.

9.

The House Morphed into a Starship

"I could see two shadowy figures walking towards me."

One night at the beginning of summer in 1974, everyone was asleep in my home. Disturbing lights began to filter through every corner of the house, including cracks and windows. Nothing was dark any more. I slowly woke up, feeling the warmth of a sunny day on my face and the intense light coming through my eyelids as if facing the sun. My brain slowly realized it was night time, and I was supposed to be asleep in my room, but I had crossed into another dimension because my thoughts echoed in my head.

"How is that even possible?"

I was fully conscious that my eyes were open and my brain was active. I got to see these amazing bright lights inside and outside the windows as if it were total day light. I noticed a bright amber light at the end of the corridor shining directly on my face.

We lived in a small family house with three bedrooms and one bathroom located six or seven meters away from my bed at the end of the hallway.

The light was so bright it hurt my eyes to look at it. I tried to gather myself, but I couldn't move from my waist down. I tried to scream, but my voice was gone. I could only make some weird sounds but not loud enough to call someone.

My house began to morph into another structure, that of a spaceship. I knew I was not alone; someone other than my family was there. My body couldn't help but tremble even though I wasn't totally scared yet. At that moment, I felt as if I were trapped in my own mind; breathing and logic started racing at the same pace as my heartbeat. I began to freak out. Then, this shadowy figure, a man's silhouette, started to drag itself in my direction.

In my head I'm thinking, "He's coming to get me. This is not a dream. I know that I am fully awake, for Christ's sake! Gee, I don't want him near me. What is this? What does it want with me?"

Oh God, I prayed the "Our Father" rapidly in my thoughts. I begged God to let me be invisible to this apparition by praying all the prayers I knew by heart. I didn't want this thing to know I was quite awake.

"I know this was a nightmare, a dream!" I thought to myself.

So, I closed my eyes very tight and opened them up slowly.

"I know this is over, I know this is over!" I tried to convince myself.

To my surprise, I opened my eyes back again and saw very clearly now.

A dude, older than I am by a few years, completely drenched in sweat and bleeding from his tummy, his hands holding the wound, was contacting me for some reason. I suppose I knew he knew I was awake. He was there looking for something and found it when he found me, but I couldn't move a finger, not because I couldn't physically, but because I knew "the others" were watching my every move.

"What was I supposed to do? It wasn't my time yet. I couldn't be of any use to them."

The guy had cinnamon red hair, wavy and down to his neck. He had freckles and a small, pointy nose. His eyes were either blue or green, or maybe hazel. He was slender, and looked around seventeen, my older brother Frankie's age. He looked away and breathed heavily, and I was still trembling and had a cold sweat. I looked down to the floor and saw blood, his blood, everywhere. A pool of blood began to form under his feet. Then he died, and I felt his last breath near me and felt his spirit detach from his weak body.

At that moment, my home was no longer a house. Somehow, I was in a starship!

"I was in it and don't know how everything happened," I thought.

I looked around carefully and at everything in detail. I didn't hear an engine or see anyone flying the craft, but I was positive it was a craft of some kind. Inside, there were hundreds of humans like me, and I was one more in the bunch. I walked into a secluded room with others who for no reason walked in with me. Every room was different. People were separated into group by ages, it seemed. All boys and girls, including me, were butt naked, and we were all together. I came to think that no one had time to realize it, and I couldn't help but have a cynical smirk on my face. No one else cared about their natural condition.

I remember asking myself why no one cared or at least showed being embarrassed by it. I guess I was the only one with that question. So, I played along. I guess everyone was doing the same.

Meanwhile, in the other room right across my path, there was an amber light just like the one I saw previously in my home, yet this one was different than the other lights. I could not see the light source of any of them, not like the ones I was used to seeing where I came from. I saw nothing like a switch, or markings of any kind, or edges on the walls. The ceiling and some walls produced their own soft white brightness.

I saw a human hand followed by a whole arm; it was hanging down from a raised bed which I saw from afar. It was a kid around my age, but I couldn't see anything anymore. I lost interest when he was taken away. I shut my eyes and could only hear in my head that he was taken back.

I remember asking myself, "Where?"

Someone said, "Don't worry about that."

And I did; I didn't care any longer.

About twenty more minutes later, I smelled an odor that came from a really huge space. I cannot describe it with any human logic. I could see two shadowy figures walking towards me. I knew they were coming for me. My body began to tremble with this uncontrollable fear. I felt shock and gasped for air. I couldn't breathe or scream either.

They operated this thing, like a medical instrument, yet more like a tool. I still couldn't see who they were exactly, but I knew they were small people, like little people, with perfect, slender bodies, skinnier than regular skinny. They put some pressure around my waist with that tool. I noticed the thing had a diamond-shaped glass on the top. They pressed it and the thing came out like a snake's forked tongue. I can't be quite sure. I felt dazed and in limbo, and I went under the most extreme sensation of peace encompassing my whole being.

The funny thing is that my mind was totally alert. I had many questions rushing through my head; my logical sense was still intact. I knew I had to be either tripping or dreaming. Little by little, they seemed more familiar to me. They looked better, and I knew I was fully alert. I had no fear anymore when I started to observe their pear-shaped head, eyes, height, arms and feet. Their heads were bigger than a regular head for their height. Their skin looked very pale. I was sure they weren't naked like the rest of the humans, but they did look like they were. They wore this silk light material from their neck down to their feet. They had boots and did not have pockets in their bodysuits. I couldn't see any zippers or gloves on their hands; at least that is what I recalled.

"Oh, nooo!"

Their hands were these strange claws like mythical monsters, little monsters.

"Oh, my God; it is scary!" I thought.

I am having all this anxiety but in slow motion, off and on. My body trembled again, and then I started to shiver. My jaw dropped, and a trickle of drool was oozing off my mouth. Although I was having these thoughts about their ugly looks, I knew we knew each other and that they thought that everything was OK, and I would be going back to my family soon. And then I felt guilty for passing judgment on their looks. I was a horrible human being for thinking such negative thoughts about their looks as if it made any difference at this point.

The House Morphed into a Starship

I focused on a set of huge, black eyes staring at me. It was one of them, another small being with a mission to stare at me. He began to manipulate some sort of a machine, but it did not have any buttons, switches, or even a lever. From there a claw-like hand resembling a bear claw twisted some wires in different ways as if they were meant to do different procedures. The wires resembled pure silver or chrome, a soft metal with tiny pores. Somehow, I moved an inch closer and had a better look.

"You don't need to know what this is; you wouldn't understand!" they said.

I stopped and cared no more.

Next, I was taken to this other room; everyone I remember was in there. I knew them! Most of them were Nordic looking, except for some small group that looked like me. There was another race of red-haired people, too. I was eyeing everyone, and then I didn't see the others like me or like other races on Earth either. I felt like a fly on a cup of milk for my dark complexion. The rest of them were all white, red or pale, yet we all shared one thought, one mind, one everything. We all had thoughts not related to the ongoing event.

I looked around and this blinding light said, "Goodnight!"

Later, I woke up in my bed totally confused as to what had just happened to me.

***

This experience was one of the most baffling ones I have ever had. Years later, I realized I actually experienced two separate phenomena.

The first one was the vision of the ghost who entered my room and died in a pool of blood right in front of me. It terrified me completely and still haunts me to this day. The

105

amazing thing was that five years later in 1979 the vision I saw of the ghost actually came true!

I had befriended a guy a few years older than me back then. We both got caught up in the infamous civil war in Nicaragua. I elected to escape the country to the USA and continue my education somehow, but my friend chose to stay behind. On the morning of my departure, I learned that my friend had been murdered in the same way as I saw in my vision five years before in 1974! The astounding thing that really blew my mind was that only then did I realize that my friend in the flesh had the exact same appearance as the ghost from five years before.

"How was this possible?" I thought to myself over and over.

Since then, I have learned that time is not what we think it is. We live in a NOW where everything is happening at the same time including the past and the future. Some of us, including myself, have access to this timeline portal where we have clairvoyant visions of the future. But five years! So incredible.

Plus, my memory had been blocked until that fateful moment of my friend's murder. I've asked myself over and over why was I shown this premonition of my friend's death.

"Why didn't I remember it so that I might have been able to save him?"

I can only conclude that this event had already happened in this mysterious NOW and that I was, again, set up to be a witness to my friend's death without knowing why. And that's the thing about so many aspects of paranormal encounters: the mind tries to figure it out but can't.

The second part of this extraordinary experience was the morphing of the house into a starship. This made the overall experience a combination of a paranormal incident with the ghost and an extraterrestrial one with the starship ... very unusual and unique indeed! Not only that: it's the way the extraterrestrial incident began with the vision of the house transposing right before my eyes.

I have later learned that my abductors had the ability to mind control me such that I think I was seeing what I was seeing when in fact it was all happening in my mind. In other words, the house was not actually being altered by a strange, piercing light and otherworldly dimensions. Instead, I was experiencing the changes superimposed on top of my reality. Then at some point during this dreamscape fantasy, I was abducted onto the starship where I interacted with all these children I described above. I'm sure that part was real as I was fully awake and in my physical body.

The question remains as to why these beings would put on such a light-and-set show for me. I have no idea. I can only guess they were giving me a warning that I was about to be abducted onto their ship.

It's also occurred to me that the paranormal incident with the ghost and the extraterrestrial incident on the ship have nothing to do with one another. Rather, the higher frequencies and dimensional portal of the extraterrestrial experience may have induced the ghost to show itself to me as if seeking some justice with me as the witness.

"But what was I to do with all this information?" I thought.

I was so traumatized at the time that I was just glad to be back in my bed and that the nightmare was over. I live with the deep sorrow that I could not have saved my friend even though I was shown his tragic destiny. What's even more horrific is that I feel I would have been prevented from saving him anyway because it would have caused some timeline violation already permanently locked up.

10.

Otherworldly Creatures

"Then, communication began. They talked to me in my mind."

It was dark back in Grandma's farm house and time to hit the sack. I was ready for bed. The little old lady always made sure we all used the latrines before going to bed when we went over for our first vacation of the year. That was *Semana Santa* and in Latin countries our governments legalized the whole week for a vacation. So, after Holy Week, which included Easter, *Semana Santa* was the second major holiday period of the year.

Grandma Gultier did not like to find herself in a rude awakening with her grandkids wetting the beds in her home. I was around 5 going on 6 years old then. My brothers and most cousins older than me were already in bed, and I had to go pee pee pretty bad.

I loved a chocolate beverage Grandma used to prepare for us called *Pinolillo*. It is a mix of cinnamon, toasted corn kernels and cocoa beans pulverized by hand. It was a refreshing, awesomely delightful drink indeed, a gift from our Mayan ancestors.

I think I had too much *Pinolillo* that night and that kept me worried because I told my grandma I was going to act like an adult if she let me spend the holidays. She never allowed anyone to do so because of having to deal with little kid's issues. When I realized I couldn't hold my urine, I went around and begged everyone, including my brothers, to keep me company while I went to the outhouse to relieve myself. No one wanted to bother with it, so I was on my own and about to explode.

I went directly to the mean, old woman, and to my surprise, she talked to me with tenderness, gave me this weird half-asleep look, and handed me a flashlight.

"You go, boy. Do not be scared of 'coco.' You're a little man. Remember that!"

She said that to me to give me courage, but it worked out the other way around since she already had mentioned coco, and I just couldn't take him off of my mind. "Coco" is what's known as the boogeyman.

Into the Dimensions

Back in the 1960s my grandparents' farm had no electric power yet. I tried to convince myself that I was a big boy and not a cowardly sissy boy. I tried to brainwash myself with that attitude even though inside of me I was trembling all over like a scared-to-death little mouse. I had to walk in the dark by myself next to the chicken house and pass some scary bushes that formed shapes of demons and other such scary characters once you pointed the flashlight at them. The wind, light and shadows formed a total Halloween type of horror gallery. My heart then raced like energetic drums playing for a life-and-death acrobatic scene in a circus show. I began my steps to get my mind away from my fears. I counted fifty-two steps from Grandma's backdoor to the outhouse. Many times, I had walked these steps by myself, but that was when there was some sunlight left and never as dark as that awful night. It was so dark that the light coming from the flashlight was not as bright.

A pungent, weird odor, like ammonia, spread throughout the air that gave me a cold sweat all over, but mostly on my hands and feet. It was like no other night I could remember before that one. What I did was a 180 degree turn from where I had advanced so far and wound up back at Grandma's backdoor and next to the manicured garden she kept in shipshape.

Grandma Gultier had a sharp hearing when anyone was in trouble or tried to hide something from her.

Suddenly, I heard her distinctive voice yelling, "Véte al excusado, no en mi jardin, oistes?!" Then, she added "Carajo!" She meant, "Go to the latrine and not in my vegetable garden, you hear?! Darn it!"

Gee, I was in trouble and that made me tenser than I already was.

She still mumbled something to me with a sleepy voice, "City boys!"

I tried to make up an excuse by replying, "What if a snake bites me?"

I said it really low; I didn't want the rest of the boys to mock me the rest of the week for acting like a little sissy boy.

I can still hear all my cousins and my brothers giggling at my own expense. It was crystal clear enough what they mumbled; I was totally ashamed of myself for being a baby about the whole thing. It was kind of weird and embarrassing at the same time.

Yet, Grandma seemed to be waiting for a satisfying response on my part, so I yelled back, "I'm going, I'm going, Grandma!"

A tear or two ran down my face; I was terrified. I knew I was risking my reputation and my butt if I ever got caught by Grandma Gultier. She could be a sweetheart, yet a mean, old lady if you defied her rules. So, I decided to walk towards the opposite corner of Grandma's room regardless of my nervousness, and I peed right up against the wall to ensure grandma's bionic ears did not catch me in the act.

Unexpectedly, something eerie and supernatural flooded my whole world. What happened next was not just physical, but also emotional—a true, unusual and strange event that I wouldn't forget for the rest of my days. I stood there frozen with fear. I then heard an unusual noise coming from the chicken coop. It was a distress call the chickens make when they feel threatened or afraid.

I began to get dazed and felt like I was living inside a slow motion movie. Time stopped. Everything around me began to feel like I was in a dream, a very odd one. I began to doubt that all of it was real and decided that I had to be in a dream. It was a bad one, of course, a nightmarish kind of dream. My whole body began to tremble unstoppably, followed by my mouth and teeth; they shook like a bag of marbles thrown against the floor.

And then there was this intense and sordid humming in the air. The winds were blowing towards it, and I heard an excruciating ringing in my ears. I wondered if that was inside my mind when I twisted in pain trying to grab my head, which felt as if it were about to split open. My whole body got rigid, and I couldn't move a single muscle.

I wanted to walk slowly to be unnoticed and then run away far, or perhaps go back inside the house and hide under the beds and let everyone else deal with it. My heart was thumping, and the night turned into daylight, as if the sun came down from the sky and stopped right above Grandma's little house.

I slowly turned my face for some unknown reason and saw what seemed to be some living creatures that resembled ghostly figures by the chicken coop! These three ghost-like beings looked like the cartoon character I watched on the TV almost daily, Casper and his friendly ghosts. It was an odd and scary situation for a little kid like me at first because, even though I was a very small child, I kind of knew Casper was nothing but a cartoon and not so real.

These ghostly figures had huge eyes wrapped around their faces with a shiny appearance and a deep black color, the darkest I had ever seen. Casper and his pals looked like kids my age, just like me, so it was easy to relate to them, yet scary at the same time.

"What sort of kids were able to have that kind of power in their hands?" I thought while mesmerized.

The beings were around my height yet formed like peculiar toy soldiers. I didn't know if they were scary to look at, or cute in some kind of strange way. At that point, I was not afraid anymore, perhaps for the heat of the moment or maybe because I felt numb. I couldn't be so sure about that anymore! I could reason that and comprehend it as well, yet my young mind got trapped between reality and fantasy. I couldn't explain it, but the concept was still there in my logic regardless of my age. I was a smart boy, you know.

My mind was fighting against this invisible force, and I was able to free myself somehow and could move a little. The first thing I did was try to control my feet, and I did. I got the feeling as if my feet were floating and dangling off the ground, and then I felt I was totally suspended in midair.

What I experienced that fateful night was so shocking to this day. The feeling was exactly as when you come out of a bad fever and you sweat it out, but you still remain dazed from the effects of the drugs and pain. The heat had intensified right on my cheeks and started to burn my sides from my neck upwards. It was dark, really dark, but I had the illusion that I had a spotlight right on my face.

Then, communication began; they talked to me in my mind. One thing I noticed was that they were not translucent like ghosts should have been. Their thoughts became my thoughts. They did not actually talk to me, but we still communicated with what I heard as voices in my head, loud and clear. They saw me as I was, not the human child everyone else saw in me, but as an intelligent living creature, just like they were. They told me that my mind was on the same level as theirs, and, therefore, we were on the same level of communication. That was so cool because human adults never cared, or seemed not to care, when I had to say what I felt, or what I wanted to do, or when I was being serious about something. These beings respected me; they respected my person; they respected my mind; they saw me like one of their own.

The three beings planted ideas in my head that I never dreamt of in my whole life. I knew I couldn't conceive of any of it on my own when I used my brain: solutions and points of views that later on in life I learned were a real issue to humanity. I understood that clearly as they did. They showed me images to communicate flawlessly with me, and I learned that our human language was ancient and undeveloped, and not advanced enough to help us move forward into the future.

I had a good feeling, but I knew it was not in a normal, earthly environment. No one ever made me feel that important in this way, especially at that age. I remember they made a deal with me, and I agreed. However, I can't remember what sort of a deal, yet I agreed. I still couldn't move; my whole body was rigid again. I felt trapped, but still sedated!!! I could only move my head and eyes, and I began to drool and release myself. I heard the noise from the urine hitting the dirt below me. My leg and shorts were soaking wet. I felt the sticky warm fluid, which suddenly turned cold when the intense light went dark in a brief second. Everything around me turned pitch black, and I was out.

"Good morning, kiddo!"

I snapped back into reality, thank God! That was a human sound, the voice of Grandma Gultier's angelical voice, thank God, yes! I felt relieved from that ugly ringing in my ears, yet I woke up with a terrible headache. I was happy my ordeal had ended. I kept wondering if all of it was just a dream, or not.

Grandma joyfully said to me with her sweet voice, "Are you hungry, boy?"

My tummy was growling. I said desperately, "Yes, Grandma!"

Then, she said something like, "What is that awful smell, for Pete's sake?"

I agreed with her that I did stink like an old goat. I totally forgot that I had peed in my shorts and on my legs. I couldn't remember all of that as if it weren't even real. I couldn't remember for years. Something in the back of my head knew I was afraid of something, but I wasn't able to figure out what that was.

"Go take a bath now before you sit at the table with the rest of the family!" she said as she covered her nose coughing in disgust.

Indeed, I did smell really bad. I looked under the sheets to see if I had an accident while asleep, but everything down there was neat and dry except for my feet being dirty. It was not any animal poop; instead, it was more similar to the smell of gunpowder and piss.

I got up and walked fast to the bathtub and washed myself, but the smell was attached to my skin. I had immediate recollections about what I thought was a dream followed by heaviness, and then I remembered barely enough about the night before. Yet my memories had holes, and so I was kind of confused. I couldn't piece it together. What a bummer!

"How did I get back to bed?"

I knew I had lived through something; I kind of knew it was not a fantasy either. I was sure of that more and more as I found strange markings on my skin and inhaled a strange acidic smell that was nothing I had ever sensed before. Soon enough, I forgot the whole thing, thank God.

Afterwards, I became more sensitive to people's emotions and thoughts.

As I was growing up, I kept asking myself more than before, "How come I can't remember what happened that night?"

It was totally unclear to me, yet I got the feeling that a star in the sky came down to Earth and talked to me, kissed me on my lips, talked to me, and then nothing. No thoughts, no clues, no answers.

***

Looking back, I now know that this experience was my first abduction by extraterrestrials because I had a missing time sequence that night, which can only mean that I was taken to a ship. I have no memory of that missing time as is typical because I'm sure my memory was wiped clean. I also know that the "Casper" beings were Short Greys, and I encountered them numerous times again in other abductions throughout my entire life.

My life become extraordinary after that experience. Soon enough, I knew I had this gift that no one else had. People got scared of my comments. Kids my age would be thoughtless and avoid my weird talk. So in order to have friends, all I had to do was to pose as an innocent, little fool and playact as such. I hated my life. I felt trapped because I couldn't have a smart conversation with kids my age, so I befriended or impressed my friend's parents with my unusual knowledge. This stressed me out because they thought I was cute and bright, but that wasn't the message I wanted to send.

"Oh, well, all I had to do was act and become what others expected of me," I thought.

I had a sad life, but in order to survive, I played their game and I was good at it!

11.

The Never-Ending Lights

"The spheres were like never-ending lights
in the sky in front of me and all around me."

Embú das Artes, São Paulo, Past Midnight

Introduction

On November 25, 2012 in my travels to South America, I visited, São Paulo, Brazil—a lovely country rich in everything you can think of. *Embú das Artes* literally translates as "'Land of the Arts," a picturesque, small arts-and-crafts town. Its streets are covered with cobblestones, some twenty-four miles from São Paulo. I was there for the Christmas holidays.

I had rented a place all to myself in a rural area outside of the town. Upon arrival in my rented car, everything seemed great until I got stuck with severe weather that kept me indoors for a few days.

On my third night in town, I slept in a chaise lounge where I watched television in the wee hours and was awakened by a rumbling thunderstorm that broke out without warning. Darkness immediately surrounded the property. Then, a loud lightning strike followed and struck a power line somewhere nearby. The strong winds carried an eerie howling and whistling that whipped against the palm trees causing them to bend almost to the ground. I turned the lights on without any luck, despite the blackout, because my reasoning had abandoned me for a few seconds.

The blinking flashes from the storm let in some light in the living room area, and on the other end of the house, there was a bright spot, so bright that it looked like fire and got me even more confused. I had to rush upstairs to see up close where that absurd brightness was coming from.

My mind had a hard time trying to figure out why that light was brighter than three suns all put together in the same spot. I was curious, and the closer I got, the weirder it became. That light illuminated the whole house for quite some time and caught my attention. Just the thought of another abduction creeped me out, and everything started spinning in my head. A feeling of anxiety and overwhelming fear attacked me. When I had these experiences in the past, these beings had always used a clever parade of illusions by using hallucinations to trick my mind about some subject, probably for some dark plan. I couldn't figure it out, but I was close to finding out. I walked cautiously, holding the staircase railing while expecting the worst in every step I made. I was blinded for a while, and quickly everything turned completely dark, and I was gone.

Depressing Sameness

On the same day around 8:30 PM, the last detonation of Mother Nature's stroke surprised me one more time. I jumped off the sofa again. I remember the thought *"Déjà vu."* Yes, it was that creepy. I looked at the time on my watch. I got my hand closer to my face and confirmed it was earlier than the night before. There were a few more power failures during that storm. I glanced at the stairs again but there was this complete darkness and silence, and nothing came out from upstairs this time. I was in denial thinking the experience never happened the night before.

There was a light switch barely visible on the wall in front of me, and I flicked it up and down without any result whatsoever. I'm usually not comfortable in the dark, so I went to search for a flashlight, maybe in the kitchen drawers somewhere. I wasn't sure of my way around the house and stumbled on a couple of pieces of furniture, cursing every time I hurt my foot. I got my hand into a couple of the drawers and got a small but deep cut on one of my fingers with what seemed like a sharp knife. That definitely made me angry, and I put the knife on the counter somewhere. Now I was bleeding, in a lot of pain and still could not see a thing. I kept cursing my bad luck with the darn knife. I knocked over some other things until I finally made it to the kitchen cabinet that contained an emergency light. I grabbed it and lit up the place. A minute later, I found some candles

119

and a huge box of giant matches, so I lit all the wax candles, four in all. Very ingeniously, I placed them forming a pathway around the main hallway in the house.

Then, I felt lightheaded and about to faint when something warm was streaming down my right forearm, but quickly turned cold: it was blood oozing out of my right index finger. I could see much clearer now. One of Grandma Gultier's tips when I was a kid was to grab some ground coffee and spread it on the bleeding wound. It helped to slow down the hemorrhaging; so I did that and was back on track almost immediately feeling very alive.

The water from the rain was spreading all over the floors and walls because I forgot to close the windows. Talk about chaos! I closed each one of them as fast as I could and tried to dry the wet floors with a towel. My heart started pumping hard when I saw what seemed like an awful ghostly face creeping out behind the kitchen window. It scared the wits out of me; my heart kept pounding so hard and gave me the impression that it was going to burst out of my chest. It was insane! This time I really concluded I was delusional when these things happened to me. I am usually asleep, about to sleep, or in a trance like state, but now I was fully alert.

A friendly dog that came with the property, named Lua, rushed to the patio door and did not bark at all. She was sniffing under the door crack instead, which was a bit strange to me. I got a hold of myself and knew that my mind was probably tricking me into this experience. I looked again defying all logic and playing it safe, Thank God, it was that caretaker woman, Xírlei. She was gathering some firewood under the roof outside the kitchen door. I gulped a mouthful of air to calm myself down. I guess I felt my body going through a paranoia attack for a few seconds while my brain realized she was a human being and not a ghost. I put my fear to the side and washed my hands. I covered the wound with a new set of bandages; it still hurt but I tried not to think about it. Lua started to bark at the window behind the dining area, and I called her to get away from there. She was making matters worse. Then Xírlei knocked on the door.

"Wait a minute please," I yelled in English and then realized she didn't speak any English, so I said, "Espera um minuto por favor!"

I opened the door to let Xírlei walk in, but she remained outside; her eyes were wide open and confused. I did not say a word to her. I was in my own world and kind of knew that. That strange looking woman talked and talked until she wore me out. I leaned right at the edge of a big window turning my back on her, but not to disrespect her or ignore her. I was hiding in my own mind, my mentally distorted mind. I was in desperate need to find the logic to all these incidents, but I knew what I was going through was in reaction to my past and countless paranormal experiences during my life.

Poor Xírlei, she was all upset and talked non-stop, and I didn't understand a single word she was saying in Portuguese. As for me, I was bogged down with all kinds of questions in my head. I was tormented trying to get help from my own sanity. My thoughts questioned my own self, then I glanced at the time on my wristwatch.

"That's impossible, for God's sake. I couldn't have slept for five hours, or could I?" I thought to myself.

I felt a stinging sensation on my neck, befuddled by such a notion. I grabbed the flashlight because I couldn't see a thing but felt like something bothered me really badly. I went to the bathroom to look for the mirror. I got a closer look at that side of my neck.

It was right there, a red lump, like a bee sting right between the side of my neck, throat and jaw. I detected a tiny, hard lump shaped like a pearl inside the skin, probably a quarter inch in diameter. The flesh around it was red and hurt.

"Probably a spider bite," I thought.

Not letting my tormented mind influence me, I wiped the stream of blood running from my nose. At first, I thought it was blood from my finger when I bled earlier, but it wasn't.

I slowly squeezed the small protuberance in my nose. It felt like a marble that came out from inside the nose channel and let out a small clear drop of something that smelled like some sort of a chemical liquid that moved loose inside the skin.

"How odd!"

I covered my neck with another bandage and went back to the kitchen. Lua came up beside me and appointed herself to be my guardian. Xírlei was still there at the door, but did not come in. She was standing in the same spot where I left her; she looked like a Popsicle. I apologized to her.

I forgot she was there to see me or say something, and I just walked out without saying anything; it was rude of me. She was giving me a peculiar look, probably thinking I was a nut. She wondered about the blood mess, including the blood on the knife lying on the counter. It was a pointy fish knife. But I could not hear her clear enough to respond. I went back into a deep state of mind and felt very distant from my reality.

I tried to make some sense about all of it, but sometimes I can't explain things to myself. I would have lost my mind already if I started digging into my thoughts. Sometimes when dealing with it, I would think that I was mentally ill, and this helped me deal with these episodes. I needed to seek professional help "pronto," especially when people wondered about my actions. I tried to recall my day and remembered now very clearly that I woke up in the middle of my sleep. It was a restless night indeed.

Within forty-eight hours of my arrival from Los Angeles, I was already pulled into this deceptive form of hallucinations that I had really grown tired of. I was seriously thinking of seeking professional help once I was back in the U.S. I thought how difficult that was just to open up to a psychotherapist and tell him or her that I was seeing things, but not as "normal" people see. I was a bit skeptical about opening up; I had never even opened up to my closest friends let alone my own family.

For almost a year now, I had not experienced anything major, but I guess I couldn't escape my fate. I was face to face with this delusion. Most of the time there were moments when they were more intense, most likely when they made their presence known by mental wave sounds. Dealing with these fantasies for decades, I thought I should know precisely how to deal with them by now, but every time they happened, it was a whole different scenario, and I'd have to find a new way of dealing with them. I felt like I was in a constant spiritual battle!

The previous night I had tossed and turned when I was almost in my deep sleep state. I had the feeling I was in midair and surrounded by this unusual warmth, somewhat cooler than the sunlight but accompanied by that damn toxic smell again. I already knew what that was, had a shortness of breath because of it, and was getting another paranoid sensation. The reasoning behind all of it was that I knew there was a purpose and I got the feeling I had no other choice but to cooperate for the sake of humanity. All the real reasoning and understanding faded away within my mind, but slowly these thoughts returned as a form of denial and missing, not only time, but chunks of memories. It was becoming very frustrating for me to deal with it on a daily basis.

I cursed again and prayed at the same time saying, "In the name of God, when is all of this going to stop?"

I did not want to keep trying to hold my sanity together any longer. I wanted all the illusions to stop. However, when my mind opens up, it gets out of control and dislodges all the repressed memories, in this case, hidden secrets, and I am forced to confront my reality, which is in front of me.

Usually, I recall more than I have to, or more than the illusions allow me to.

I want to forget the whole thing like in cases that I've read where they have to go under regressive hypnosis, but not me. I was fully aware and cannot confide in many people as they would judge me or crucify me without mercy.

A vivid memory surfaced in my mind. I remembered I sensed there was more than one being passing physical inspection on me, maybe more than two. On the back of my shoulders and down my legs all the way to my feet, there was a crawling sensation of weird hands and a discussion over my health. I sensed it and understood that my time was in their hands. They expressed to me indirectly that I had to live a healthier life.

"What do I want of this life anymore? Living like a caged animal in my own world and with a limited freedom, why do I need to care?" I thought to myself.

These paranormal and extraterrestrial beings don't understand my point of view or the way I see things. I kind of see an analogy in my head about animals in the wild when conservationists trap them to monitor their health and procreation in their own territory. They mean no harm but are still violating these animals and causing them great fear and upset. These animals have no say in the decisions of the conservationists. It is exactly the way I feel when these paranormal and extraterrestrial beings abduct or intrude upon us humans. They know they are violating humans, but they're also doing their job. I would really appreciate if they left me alone, but they tell me it doesn't depend upon me. Despite the fact that we are all in this together as one race, one family and one world, they still can't honor our borders and divisions and how we think of others when we don't see them as equal.

As I am facing down, I have my eyes open, but I cannot move a finger. I can feel a drool escaping my lips but cannot catch it in time.

"Great, let them have it, one more thing for them to analyze," I smiled thinking cynically.

I was in an off mode kind of situation feeling the need not to be interested in their opinion, and it made it hard for me to even use my normal human capability to think. Then my whole body started to spin slowly in a circular motion and "*bang*," I was back in my bed with the feeling of getting knocked out. It was exactly as if I was drained of my own energy and had totally forgotten about the experience momentarily. I would have these dreams, never-ending dreams, that lasted for a while. I could remember every single detail; I knew and learned something from them; I became more illuminated than before.

And then, normally, my day would start again, and I survived without having any traumatic issues. I was convinced it was only a nightmare or some eerie dream. With whatever true memory was left in me, a few days later the trauma was over. My human capability healed the emotional and spiritual wounds, and I became normal again. I woke up and thanked Jesus it was only a dream within a dream, I would like to think. It was as if I had walked with my wondering eye into a mysterious realm, only to be pulled by the glowing lights.

On a new day with a sunny smile, I woke up and turned the TV on while I took a bath. I was listening to some news and repeating in Portuguese some of the easy words. Locals still saw me as a tourist. I think my accent was not usual. They kept asking me where I was from. They couldn't locate my appearance and I liked that. I had a reason to practice my Portuguese, although some think I was Brazilian, so funny.

Embú das Artes is a small town full of beautiful little stores where they sell handmade decorative pieces. They have a tradition every weekend of holding an arts and crafts fair, including great food. Sundays is the best day usually, but this day was a Friday. I took off to get to town. It was very warm and sunny for a change. I bought a bottle of cold water to hydrate; I was sweating a lot and took a couple of gulps to rest for a short while as it was a long walk.

While I tried to catch my breath, I saw this woman riding her bike in the narrow streets around the plaza with her kinky hair beaten to the sides by the wind. I thought she could be none other than Xírlei, the caretaker. She was acting all crazy, talking to a couple of dissidents who were drinking and hanging around the fair grounds. She was carrying *Coronel*, a little white dog with curly hair, in the small basket in front of her bike.

She got closer to a drunkard who was talking to another guy; they seemed to know each other very well. They were very effusive in their encounter; there were lots of hugs, two kisses on their cheeks, and lots of smiling. Regardless of the commotion and the multitude of people, her voice overshadowed everyone's in the crowd.

"Oi," she said.

One guy replied, "Olá. Tudo bem."

I could hear part of their conversation and laughs a mile away. The guy seemed to offer her a sip of a huge bottle covered with a brown paper bag. I was near a bench and sat there for a while as she got off her bike, desperately grabbing the bottle from her acquaintance. The man gladly let go of his precious elixir to share it with his friend. She then juggled the *Pinga*—a popular hard liquor—a cheap *Brazilian schnapps*. The wide-mouth bottle was in her possession, and she kept it upright in her mouth for almost a minute, just like an experienced drunk would do. I thought that it was funny. I smiled thinking cynically that she had no shame to do that in public. It was hilarious! I looked to the long road downtown, as I was still catching my breath, and decided that I couldn't care less about their business.

They both said their goodbyes to the other guy, Tcháu, and I got curious when they looked very suspicious at me. She had a large flour sack tied to the rack of the bike. She untied the heavy sack, and they walked away from people towards a nearby alley. Their figures receded to tiny specks on the plane. I got curious over their strange behavior and decided to follow them for the heck of it. I kept a safe distance and acted like a total Sherlock.

They both entered an old, abandoned, colonial-style house. I got closer to the tall doors that were left slightly and unintentionally open, so I thought. I pushed them just a little, and they screeched louder than I expected. I stuck my head inside and saw a long-neglected gallery with lots of brushwood growth everywhere. What else would you expect in an old, abandoned house? I thought it was too much, so I decided to desist with the pursuit; I did not like the way it was turning out. There was no sign of them. There was no way out and nothing more to see.

"How odd?" I said to myself.

However, my intuition was pulling me to go inside further, just by mere curiosity. The feeling was getting stronger than my embarrassment if they caught me inside looking for them. Yet, I decided to just go away. It was genuinely spooky, and while I was stepping back and a part of me was still on the sidewalk, a bright light swallowed me whole.

I glanced up at the sky, and it was filling up with a thick dark cloud on top of that old house with what seemed like pulsating amber lights with a bluish halo around it. I started experiencing the usual adrenaline rush and entered the usual trance.

Then, I saw *Embú das Artes* in another time and place. I heard a voice of a beautiful woman with a Hindu appearance. Her skin was totally dark; she was very pleasant to look at and possessed an extreme beauty. We engaged in an odd conversation as if we had already been talking for a while. She did not speak to me in Portuguese but in my own native Spanish.

"How did she even know?" I wondered.

She explained to me about the many civilizations before my time especially from a long time ago with origins on Earth. They were known as the *Orishas.* I had no idea they were entities like gods used by the saints in Brazil and practiced by the African slaves in the time when they were forced to become Christians or else. Not only that, but they existed in the flesh and, according to their worshipers, guided humans that asked them for favors or those who honored them.

They told her I was supposed to be a witness of many things and my destiny was already planned for me. All I had to do was stop fighting back, or otherwise I'd become very ill.

She started to sing songs. Some bugles were being played by a male figure that had the same resemblance as her, but I could not see that clearly. Another figure of a woman came out of nowhere singing and playing a very strange musical instrument like a trumpet, which sounded more like a vocal sound. She had an elongated face with very round eyes, and her skin was very pale and leathery as I observed her from where I was standing. The musical instrument was made out of some sort of soft metal, but it was very brilliant, and her hands were very slim with very long fingers.

Then, there was some sort of fire in the middle, like in between them and me. The fire had a human likeness. It started waving, and it turned into flames of fire. They rose up and down and had human movements. It definitely caught my attention.

From that very fire some forms were taking shape and started walking out with very bright bodies like human souls. They circled the fire, and one showed itself to me and told me their names. It was a formal introduction, like the same way humans do. I could not determine if they were male or female. They wore a very light tunic which covered their light bodies. I was shown many dimensions within dimensions of spiritual worlds. It was more like a history class. Some were stories of survival. Other stories were about wars in different timelines on this very planet we call Earth. There were stories of courage of our own humanity, and they told me clearly that our souls are the same, but our bodies have been modified.

What I was shown was a variety of mankind-like creatures that are spread out in the vast universe and are using Earth to serve a purpose. There are also negative forces with dark intentions turned against us for we have become a race of betrayers. It is hard to understand that humans were planted here to be natives to this world but only in captivity.

What does this mean? It means that we were placed here to pay for a crime we committed. Now, in order to survive in this realm, we were expatriated from our real carriers and body forms; we were given these forms and shapes—"a human suit"—in order to survive this atmosphere. Our bodies are limited, asleep, and jailed to serve this purpose, yet, humans understand that something is not right and that this is not our story. That is why many conscious humans still retain these remembrances of their true identities. Therefore, many of us are experiencers, seers, and are spiritually and psychically gifted.

Earth is a big trap. That's why we can't achieve the impossible, although we could only if we pulled through together, but our ego and selfishness are in the way. Our souls are infinite, and before Earth, we served other purposes of a higher level. Now we need to break free, but we are stuck and only by dying can we free ourselves. It's sad but true because we are hard headed and can't see what historic men of renown have seen.

Although we have an infinite desire to survive, we are not allowed to experience it. We need to pay the price because we broke The Source's trust to become eternal and transcend throughout the veil of mystery, which is consumed by our nature. We were given tools by The Source within our structure for many purposes: survival, the need to belong, and the drive to fight back against injustice and slavery.

Having a family and feeling attached to them, a wife or a husband, children, parents, etc., traps and consumes us. It stops us from seeking what our infinite spirit's true desires are. It is complicated and hard to understand. The wish for power, riches, and fame are built within our minds just to hold us back even more, to keep us aligned to serve "their purpose," meaning the dark forces who control us. Nothing is new under the sun and is the sordid echo constantly nagging in my head.

That night, I traveled in the spirit through many universes filled with color and light. I had a light body formed by energy and plasma of some kind. I felt every little tingling sensation, sound, and visual impression allowed in this body form. I was glad and thankful I could retain my mind and my thoughts. I went through things and around things. These things were shapes called doors and dimensions. Besides an agglomeration of knowledge, I felt an understanding that became me. I had the essence of wisdom, and that force stayed with me throughout the whole experience. I was joyful and overly happy to learn that we are more to this human form than meets the eye. How wonderful! We are infinite and whole. One of the secrets I learnt was that wisdom, love and communion are mandatory, and there's no way you can turn away from it or wish not to receive it. You just can't. It becomes us. We become one in that dimension, which is our true identity. What turns men against each other is the limited comprehension of complicated spiritual laws that we are supposed to live by.

At this point, I can only compare my brain to a scanning machine with a video camera attached, and many thoughts and memories were downloaded into my mind. I was not really scared, but I was in fear for knowing too much. I guess they knew that, but I was chosen to learn about that regardless. The vision in the park was only to call my attention into bringing me to that secluded place. When they were done, they just vanished into that fire or portal. I felt as if my brain was completely fried.

Then, I saw this man with a human likeness. His skin was very pale, but I knew he used to be one of us, human that is. He had a really evil spirit walking along with him, and it was his guide. No one said anything—a total silence. A voice in my head warned me to stay away and ignore any type of contact.

He observed me carefully. I couldn't stop him from doing that. He was some sort of a spirit, and his soul was tainted with innocent blood. How did I know these things? I still cannot say.

Next, I was back in a slow motion-like state.

The evil spirit referred to me.

"He is one of them," he said.

I was trying to avoid the man and his evil spirit, or ignore them, but when the man tried to come closer to me, he let out a loud sound that came from within, like a herd of pigs that had been butchered. I felt a strong energy coming out of me, and he was gone, followed by the evil one who was his guide.

It was as if a flash of light constantly follows my eyes; it turns off and on like a switch every time I detect any paranormal activity nearby.

The chanter called me by my middle name, and I obeyed quickly turning to her. She said things to me that I have forgotten over the years. I wondered how in the world she could know all of those things about my life. It was a challenge to be there with a straight face when I know I have never seen this person or being, and it is real, right in front of me, and is having some form of communication with me. I was reluctant to keep listening but could not do anything; I was there until the end. She explained that she needed my total attention.

"We're one—listen up! We're one mind, one spirit. We're one."

She explained that her mission was to encounter me at that exact time and that seeing the caretaker and the drunk was only an excuse to motivate me to follow them to get all this information.

I asked her, "What am I supposed to do with all this information anyway? Are you evil?"

She did not reply.

My gut feeling was telling me that she was not evil, but just another mystery the universe had to offer me.

She then used telepathy with me. Think and boom! All these memories came as fast as the power of thought, and I knew I had done my job now transferring these messages, for good or for evil, yet that was the purpose. I also understood that I was another messenger in my own time.

My experience with this Hindu woman seemed like memories transferred into my brain on another plane of thinking, just like a cascade of strong waterfalls flowing nonstop into me. The experience was a main source of wisdom that overwhelms my spirit every time I recollect it. I was a new me, a god! Nothing in this world gave me that certainty until my third eye opened up, the spiritual eye that co-exists within us and our souls. I was able to come and go as I pleased. I was in many places at the same time; I was here and there; I was everywhere. Nothing stopped me; nothing detained my full intension to experience the intangible, yet, my intentions were the right choices in my new body, my new space, my new me.

Wow, no experience had been as great since the day my mother gave birth to me. I wanted to come into this world and was very anxious to become a man and do great things. I wanted to love and be loved. I wanted to do good and befriend every human, every animal, every insect, anything with life. Oh God, what have I done with my life? How far have I strayed from the mission I was entrusted? I look back

132

and my true way has been broken into so many pieces. There's no way I can glue it all back. All I can do at this point is to stop producing pain and sorrow. I think I can still fix my ways from now on, but it won't be easy. My ego and my anger are still part of me when I see human injustice and misery.

Now her eyes blinked immediately after she switched from one language to another.

I couldn't just run the hell out of there. I was stuck but did not want to be there anymore. I was very anxious but not scared, although I was not too happy either. Somehow, I felt that I had already decided and had no choice but to follow through with it until the end of my ordeal.

A very skinny and pale guy came in. He was very much human looking, but I knew he was a hybrid. His eyes were very round and full, and his skin resembled the Greys in some way. I cannot remember the color of his eyes. At first, it was a bit intimidating. I knew they were colored, but some shadow was covering most of his appearance.

I remembered him; somehow my mind raced like I knew him from somewhere. Yeah, right from junior high school and I smiled. He was telling me to not be afraid.

Just as if he were inside my mind, he said to me without moving his lips, "Long time no see."

I agreed, did remember him, and replied with a simple, "Yeah."

He showed me in my mind our first encounter. It was when I somehow was taken from my elementary school; I was in third grade around eight years old. I was gone for at least five hours; my folks were going crazy thinking the worst. I nodded, and he put his warm and very slim, weightless hand on my shoulder. Immediately, I felt this soothing feeling. I looked around and the lady was gone. Now it was he and I and a couple of other beings standing right behind me. In my head, I was thinking to look behind.

"You're not allowed," a voice in my head said.

And so, I didn't.

I felt somehow embarrassed to know this being could read my thoughts.

He continued, "They are here just to learn, but they have no authority to engage in any sort of contact with you."

I felt that they stepped back a few inches away from me, and now I could not even see their shadows or feel their radiation either. Just like medicine, the thought about them vanished, and it did not bother me any longer that they were behind me. My curiosity was gone instantly. I tried not to think. I usually wonder about anything and everything, but at this moment, it was one thing at a time.

I reminded myself, "Baby steps, boy!"

I think I was more prepared than before to interact with these beings. It was not easy, and as a human, we always have the same questions and the same fears in the back of our heads. We question ourselves about who they are, what do they want, and what is the great idea about keeping secrets? Damn, at that moment I knew all the answers, but when I am in my own realm I easily forget. Why can't I remember in detail?

"Oh well, *c'est la vie!*"

Still I thought, "What's with the veil of mystery? Their whole **CHARADE?!**"

This time it was rather strange. For the first time, I was interested in acting out my free will. No one is guiding me. I didn't feel any sort of pressure nor a feeling of alienation or someone else's thoughts pushing against mine. I was feeling I could think on my own and discuss it. I would like to know what this experience was all about. The strange pale guy did not frighten me for some reason. He was more like someone who really cared about my well-being, and I sensed that, so I felt a bonding there.

One thing that was revealed to me this time was that there is a plan, and many others and I are part of that plan. It is hard to explain in words and goes beyond this life that the world is not exactly what we think it is. On a few occasions, I hear "humans make everything so difficult," and I wonder. These beings consider that everything we know and learn is being tampered with and that many of us are already contaminated. One of the reasons for these experiences, or so-called abductions, is for them to make sure that the level of contamination is kept under control. Otherwise, the contamination is like a spreading disease.

There is an issue communicating with our race to really understand the purpose of their interest or the motives of their guardianship, so understanding was a level I needed and had acquired. I can say that I do understand it but cannot explain it with words, even in my native language. Perhaps it is because I was mediocre in my school years, and honestly, I don't know why they picked me. I know many good candidates better than I to go through this.

"Pick anyone but me!"

For years, I was in constant contact with them, and through telepathic waves that are perceived by something they taught me to use over the years of training. This is the way it was originally intended, but it was protected to be used only with them on their terms and should not be tampered with. Our creation as a whole should be all in constant communication and spiritual evolution with the rest of the universe for we are all a part of it, and somehow it is dormant in our minds. But instead, we are preoccupied with taking all our time trying to outsmart everyone and fulfilling a life of empty successes that has no real value at the end of our journey.

"Humans!"

I opened my eyes and was back in the middle of the commotion of the weekend fair, sitting on that park bench. I looked up and the sky had darkened. A few drops of rain started falling on my head. I looked at the time, and it was already around 3 PM. That was a sign for me to go back home with a fresh mind. I stopped by the bakery shop and got myself a ton of sweets, desserts, fresh ham, cheese and those delicious Brazilian French rolls. I did not feel like getting soaking wet again, so I took the bus *Via Avenida Joao Batista.* I kept thinking about the experience, and it felt very positive. I could not remember all the details either, which in a way was good, but then frustrating because I had it all in my mind, but not in detail or in order. Later on, the questioning started all over again.

"How in the world did I get from point A to point B?"

I don't recall clearly. I knew it was kind of a hallucination, or maybe not? I had these scary thoughts that I was schizophrenic. I thought about it for years; my mind was leading me on with all this nonsense. I wanted out. I felt everyone was staring at me in the bus, a conspiracy of some sort.

"Were some of those non-humans watching my every move?"

I put it out of my mind as usual and looked away from people, forcing my eyes on the cloudy sky. Then, *"bang,"* there it was! I saw it through the glass windows: a sphere the size of a basketball and bright like the very sun rushing through the uphill woods. It was following us, rushing at the same speed of the bus.

I looked at everyone to see if I could have any witnesses, but everyone was, to my mind, moving in slow motion and looking away. I felt heavy and tired. The bus was not moving either. When the bus physically stopped, *"bang,"* I was in this reality again.

A very pretty, young woman sitting next to me asked me, "Tudo bem, senor?" (It meant: "You all right, mister?")

"Sim tudo bem," I nodded and forced a smiled.

People in back of me stared.

I probably acted strange. I don't know, but I recall I was hesitating about the whole thing, so I tried to calm down and close my eyes all the way to my stop. That was embarrassing. I swear they probably thought I was on drugs.

136

When I got out, it was pouring, and I rushed into the house. I was damp from head to toe. I opened the gates with the remote control and waited under the gate's roof a couple of minutes for the rain to slow down. Then, I ran into the house. My guardian dog followed me, and I let her in with me. Soon after, I changed into dry clothes and laid down on the couch to put my feet up just for a short time. The dog shook all the water off her fur and got me wet.

"Damn, Lua, you got me all wet!"

She couldn't care less.

I placed a towel next to her to lie on.

Xírlei then walked by the open window and asked if I was all right, "Oi. Tudo bem?"

"Sim tudo muito bem."

She asked me if I needed anything. The caretaker was going into town because she had a real emergency. I didn't want to ask her if I could help because the emergency was probably something very private. So, I just nodded and forced a smile, but she kept mumbling something to herself and looking up at the clouds. She walked away grabbing her bike and pulled out something from her pockets. I couldn't help but giggle when I saw her tearing off a big black garbage bag to use as a raincoat. She was going down to town regardless of any more rain; she called for Coronel, her little white pooch, and placed him in her basket, and they took off.

I went to my computer and probably took at least an hour to write everything down so I wouldn't forget the details I remembered. I didn't get up until I finished my story. The window that oversees Xírlei's apartment was right next to where I plugged my laptop into the wall to get Internet access. Lua came looking for me; she barked at the window, calling me to go outside and play fetch with her for a while, which I did. I threw the ball, sticks and plush toys; she loved it. The other dogs (five in total) came to join us in the game.

I was still playing with the dogs outside when the big wooden gates slowly opened. Xírlei was back, riding her old bike, and she looked a bit tipsy. Coronel jumped out of the basket, barking and running towards me, and the other dogs in the front yard area, while moving his little, curly, white tail and greeting all of us. Xírlei placed her bike in the parking spot under her apartment and grabbed a small but heavy bag out of the basket, which she protected from the rain with another plastic bag. She slipped and landed on the damp stone floors, and most of the contents of the bag wound up on the wet grass. A couple of beer bottles rolled away. She was upset and damned her luck.

"PORRA!" She yelled! ("Damn it," she said.)

She reached for a small smashed box that looked like a pack of smokes and tried to fix it by blowing some air onto them, as if that would revive them (very comical, indeed). Then, she chased after the beer bottles and kept dropping them back down on the ground.

I turned the light off so she wouldn't see me; I did not want to embarrass her. I think she didn't notice me anyway. She finally was able to grab her things and disappear inside her apartment slamming the door.

"A real emergency, indeed," I thought.

I went straight to bed; I was getting drowsy. It was a restful evening; everything was completely calm at this point. I got up the next day and this time drove my rented car to Sao Paulo. I love to drive far and wide. My mind clears up, and I find inner peace often. In my trip to the city, I kept wondering if my mind was playing tricks on me. Inside my head, I had only one thought which kept screaming "schizophrenia." I was afraid that the nightmare would start all over again, and I would see what others can't see.

Epilogue

When things like that happened to me, what I did was try to deny it and toss it away from my mind as far as I could. I always tried to find a logical answer to these anxieties. I'm sure they were the result of sleep deprivation because I know I don't sleep enough. I am always involved in these experiences that drain my energy and turn into a vicious cycle.

I have learned to survive and accept these experiences without hesitation for they're part of my life. They're not easy to deal with and not a welcoming feeling either. I have no control over them. It does not always happen, and they do not come at will. I try to keep a straight face when I'm in the middle of a crowd every time I see monsters. Most of the time they live inside ordinary, regular, everyday people. It is always about keeping the sanity of my mind and the reasoning, otherwise I would be lost. At this point in my life, I am not going to give up without a fight, but some other times I lose my strength and these battles. It is also about jumping from one realm into another without any clues and so quickly that I can't even keep up anymore!

As usual, I had a great time in São Paulo. Returning to **Embu das Artes**, lightning struck miles away in a thunderstorm. In the distance, the lightning looked like electric towers, but I wouldn't know. I kept my eyes on the heavy traffic, which is an everyday issue in that city. It moved an inch at a time, and I couldn't believe the rain was getting stronger by the minute like the horrid rains in Miami where I lived for many years. It took me at least forty-five minutes just to get out of the downtown area. Then, I took the **Rodoviaria Via Embú**. The rain slowed down, but the sky grew darker by the minute; black clouds filled the sky everywhere. I looked up at a certain point, and "**bang**," there were countless, luminous, weird-looking spheres of strange shapes dancing in the sky. It's as if they could read my mind.

I felt pulsating waves pounding my temples and the sensation of being in a sordid world. My brain began to feel a pressure as if I were being scanned. The spheres were like never-ending lights in the sky in front of me and all around me.

I still do not see faces, yet I feel the leathery skin, the four hard nails like claws, and also a feeling of being ignored by these beings when I try to make some sense with them. It is a terrible feeling of dissociation. I do not know how to describe it, but it feels like I was an object to them.

Or maybe it is the other way around: they are objects to us. It is a rather uncomfortable and awkward feeling. There's no show of emotions on their part, nor courtesy to ask me first if I would accept their procedures so that I wouldn't have to go through all that traumatic drama. But probably it is a matter of pragmatism to them. As long as there's no button to push to deactivate "my hallucinations," my body knows and prepares for a routine for every occasion when all the symptoms of an alien encounter overcome me. The routine is always for my body to become stiff like a rock. It begins to tremble with this uncontrollable fear, accompanied by a cold sweat in my hands, then heavy breathing, and a rush in my head filled with many thoughts (not my thoughts). I hear them all at once in my head, and then levitation takes over.

12.

The Unlikely Hitchhiker

"I actually saw Colton's body start to
glitch and dematerialize right next to me."

LOS ANGELES, CA, 1985

When I was in my early twenties, I liked to drive at a high speed on the Los Angeles freeways. I paid countless, expensive speeding tickets but was still too young to care. Those days are in the past, thank God. I was a total fool and really didn't think too much about the consequences of my mistakes. For my friends and me, we began to party on Friday nights. There was this famous nightclub spot called Florentine Gardens in the Hollywood area, right off the 101 FWY N. I was still cruising around 10:30 PM because the later you showed up the more fun you were able to enjoy.

I had the top down in my 1982 Fiat Spider convertible, letting my long, curly hair surf in the wild waves of the air blown by the speed of my ride. I kept her in the best shape, super clean in and out and without a scratch; I was on top of her maintenance. I was often the kind of guy who liked to make new friends, especially those who liked my radical behavior.

Other times, I was rather on my own for many years when I moved in different directions and tried to avoid any attachments. I was tired of most people's dramas or having to explain myself. Los Angeles is exactly that kind of city, a cosmopolitan epicenter where you could make lots of friends in one night and the next morning can't remember what happened, but you went on with your life. I was ready for all kinds of actions and adventures. I was both fearless and careless, and that is what made me tick, so to speak. I had a lot of disposable friends back in those days because normal people just wore me out, and I wanted to avoid all the baggage that comes with those kinds of relationships.

While getting in and out of the freeway system, there were hitchhikers like pests around the LA area, but it was not my intention to pick anyone up, not in my neatly kept car, not with my new carpets, no way. I just passed them by without making any eye contact, so I did not have to feel guilty. The reason being was I felt drawn to be nice about it, but I'd rather ignore them even if they looked like nice people. I decided to get a very attractive looking car to match my personality as a wild partygoer. I felt that it was an injustice to put a hitchhiker's dirty or smelly huge backpack on my seats. I was repelled by the thought of someone who's been walking for hours producing a foul smell while sitting down on my nice, New Zealand sheepskin seat covers.

"No sir, I wouldn't have it like that."

I was carefree and ready to rumble. On that specific Friday night, nothing was going to stop me from having fun —the kind of fun I always had most weekends on those Hollywood nights. The '80s were some of the best years for me to party hardy and do all that stuff that makes young, wild people like me feel alive.

I arrived and painfully allowed the parking valet to take care of the precious crown jewel of my possessions. I looked around as if I were expecting something inexplicably different that night, perhaps something I could feel in my gut that would be forever remembered and very special to me. Then, I walked inside to let my spirit loosen up a little.

Quickly, I met with the regulars, known people who were there week after week. We knew each other only by nicknames. I wore my black leather jacket and pants with my matching cool dancing shoes. I had it going on. I was more than ready to make my moves on the dance floor. I knew I looked cool back then with my full mane of curly black hair. I was a wild cat and felt like a movie star. Once inside, I danced the night away with countless, crazy, fun girls, and we drank a lot of beers without any remorse. With just a few drinks down my throat, anyone and everyone was my friend for that night. I was the coolest Latino on the dance floor. How did I know that? Chicks danced with me when I asked, and it paid off. Those were the times in history when drinking and driving was not a hideous crime like it is now. Otherwise, I would have been jailed and fined many times or had my driver's license rebuked at some point. However, I never drove crazy when I was drunk nor exceeded the speed limit either. I knew my limitations. Once inside the nightclub, I was the king of the jungle, but once outside, the magic was over, and I turned into who I really was, a tamed, indoor cat.

The party was over at 2 AM, and I was not quite where I wanted to be yet. I was not ready to hit the sack either. The night was young, but everyone seemed tired. No one I had met wanted to go to the after-hours bars on that specific night. Gee, what are the odds? It's never happened before. That was so unfair to me. I needed to wear off my adrenaline rush.

"Damn, one of those days," I thought to myself while feeling distraught.

I had no choice but to drive up to the next after-hours spot in LA, so I turned in my valet ticket and got my nice ride back. As I drove off from that darn place, a huge crowd walked down the street to fetch their cars or to catch a ride. I drove down towards Hollywood Boulevard.

A stranger stood up from amongst the crowd. I thought I knew the guy. I guess he sat in the bar with me sometime during my break for drinks with all the girls. We were drunk and laughed together about foolish stuff. The guy was a blonde dude with long hair. He wore a cool biker's leather jacket and now was trying to hitch a ride with the wrong crowd.

When I drove by, he yelled, "Hey, man!"

"Oh gosh, no!" I thought.

I tried to avoid him but stopped anyway. Maybe I thought he just wanted to say, "Hi." I did not want to have to compromise and drive this guy anywhere for any reason at all. It was kind of boring giving someone a lift while I could be driving to have more fun somewhere else.

Then, I remembered his name: Colton. He was a nice guy, but I thought I had to lose him somehow.

144

I parked on the side of the road, keeping my engine running. Colton came rushing up to me—zigzagging in his steps. He seemed tipsy perhaps from the drinks we had at the bar.

"Dude, oh man, I knew it was you!"

I thought to myself, "What the hell?" Yet, I replied with a simple, "Wassup, man?" Oh nooo! I hated myself for that.

"Dude, can I hitch a ride with you?"

I tried to avoid doing that guy a favor by coming out with some excuse, and I immediately said, "Yes." Oh nooo, not again!

There was an awkward pause between us.

"Well, I don't know how far you wanna go in my direction."

He smiled and said, "You don't need to go anywhere to drop me off. Wherever you're going is fine with me. I'm going in the same direction."

"What? How do you know if where I live is in your direction?"

"Ventura, right?"

What? My mind raced with many questions, and I recalled we never had this conversation.

"How do you know where I live, dude?"

He pointed at the sticker on the back of my car: Ventura College.

We both laughed!

"And your name is Carlo, right? I heard someone call you that back at the club."

I nodded and laughed again.

"Colton, right?" I said to him.

"Yeah, you got it, man."

"The night is young. I'm going to hit an after-hours somewhere around Hollywood. I can't just give it up at this time; it's too early."

He smiled and said, "I'm cool with that bro; let's go."

I thought, "Let's go? What does he mean?"

But then he was charming and cool, so I leaned over to open the passenger's door.

He, too, leaned over the window and said, "I know where you are coming from, dude. I'm with you, man, and this party ain't over yet, right?"

"Right," I said.

He got into my small brown beauty. I had the top down because in Hollywood you have to act and look cool all the time. We both had a hearty laugh because he knew I was a poser.

"How about Gino's II?" Colton pointed out.

I was amazed; I was thinking the same thing. I always ended up going to Gino's II near the intersection of Santa Monica Boulevard and Vine Street.

"I love Gino's, but I dislike waiting in line."

Colton smiled with a spark in his dashing blue eyes as he said, "Don't worry, dude. I can get us in, no problem!"

"Are you for real?" I said doubting him for a moment.

"Trust me, dude. VIP pass. You'll see; let's go!" He lifted his hands up in the air and held them like a jet flying through the sky.

We drove through Hollywood and passed by the wildest and noisiest nightclubs. We saw a couple of after-hours bars right off Sunset Boulevard with long lines of people standing there. I always thought people were stupid to wait in line. Nothing was good enough for me to stand in line, so we kept on the lookout for other places in case he would be talking crap, and we wouldn't be able to make it into Gino's II. I really did enjoy Colton's company regardless of whether he got us in or not. So far, he was a cool dude, and we had so much in common already. I was considering him an investment for the party magnet position. We made a great team together. Girls usually are more likely to be drawn to us for Colton's looks. He was the hot guy; I was the brain. At least, that's what I thought.

146

We arrived at Gino's II, and the place was fully packed, as usual. There was a huge crowd standing in line, and we had zero chances of getting in. Although that night was tough on my wishes to keep on partying, I had this intuition that we wouldn't have any issues at all. There were more people than ever, and to my knowledge, the bouncers stopped letting anyone in just before we arrived.

Soon, a chubby dude dressed in really cool clothes arrived in an awesome-looking, 1950's Chevy. He also had a hat on with a set of red robin feathers stuck around the edge by his temple on the left side. He walked in with some pretty amazing-looking girls, one on each arm. He could've been a famous movie star for all I knew. The huge, pumped dudes let them in, rolling down a figurative red carpet so that the dude and his hot chicks could walk into the place like royalty.

Colton told me to keep a few steps away, so he could go charm "these dudes" as he called them. To my amazement, the giant man who stood by the main door gave him a high five followed by loud laughter. I was trying to make some sense of the whole thing, but I was pulled by my jacket and lost myself in my thoughts. That was Colton, with a wide smile on his face.

We got in with the chubby dude and his girls. Looking closely at them, his women seemed just a few years older than I was. Colton seemed to be in his early twenties just like me, and the chubby guy was perhaps in his late twenties, a hip, Greek-looking dude neatly dressed in fancy clothing. Minutes later, I heard the girls calling him Nico. He wore a three-piece black suit with fine lines of white straps and a smile slapped on his face.

"Hey guys, give me a hand with these ladies, would you? They are a handful."

"What, was that a dream?" I thought to myself, not believing my ears.

At first, I thought that Colton was joking with us, but he quickly jumped in and asked the blonde girl to the dance floor. He walked by, and I knew what he was going to say just by looking at the twinkle in his eye.

He whispered, "Learn from your master," and smiled cynically.

Wow, he really had the moves, and soon enough they were making out and desperate for each other. Darn, he was fast! I had to hurry up and learn for real. The other girl was so cute; she looked Asian, but I could not guess which country. The chick had a little accent, so I asked her where she was from, and she simply replied Japan and that her name was Tae.

"All right Tae, would you care to dance?" I happily giggled for such great luck when I thought my luck was doomed for the night.

I couldn't spot Nico in the crowd any longer. How odd that was! I wondered about that for a second but later couldn't care less where Nico went. We were having the time of our lives!

Then, a while later, I saw Nico again; he was in a private booth. He truly was the life of the party that night. He was talking to other beautiful women while he puffed on a cigar, one you could see he tasted happily. Nico bought rounds of drinks for all of us, yet he wasn't drunk to even guess he would waste money like that. Drinks kept coming to us wherever we stood or went. He seemed to be someone with lots of money and enjoyed sharing it with us strangers. He was the kind of guy who liked to make those around him happy.

Colton, on the other hand, was the kind of guy who kept you smiling from beginning to end.

A thought suddenly struck me, "What kind of a guy was I?" I didn't want to dwell on it but was curious about these kinds of things once in a while.

"Tae, what was the deal with Nico?" I asked her.

148

She looked at him over her shoulder.

He probably guessed I was wondering about their relationship and smiled at her blowing a big cloud of smoke.

Tae moved her fragile fingers in response to his gesture and said very nicely, "Nutting, we're just friends. That's all!"

What did it matter? I was having fun thanks to Colton. Tae went on explaining a little bit that they went to college together. Colton was still kissing on Mackenzie, the blonde girl with Nico and Tae. Mackenzie was from North Dakota, so she said, but she had sort of an accent in her speech. Either she was faking an accent, or she was an American as much as I was an Italian.

Tae put her arms around my shoulders very tenderly. We made out in a dark spot right on the dance floor. We also got passionate for at least five long songs in a row.

My constant dancing and grabbing Tae was getting me excited, and I was letting all my wild, compulsive nature out in the open. The Japanese princess pulled a tiny, yellow bottle out of her small, scarlet purse, opened it, and sniffed it on each side of her nostrils. I thought it was cocaine. I heard about drugs, but I was daring in my youth and didn't care. To me that was her business.

"Do you wanna try?" she asked me.

My reaction was that I doubted for a few seconds. I did not want to, but I was already in the mood for anything; I didn't want to be a party pooper. So, I nodded with a nervous smile, and she put the poison in my shaky hand and giggled. I didn't know what my reaction was going to be.

"Awright," she added.

I sniffed it twice. It was a little vial with a yellow tag and very deceiving looking. At first, I felt that my nose was breathing a sweet fire. It was a penetrating sort of chemical that smelled more like a mixture of Clorox and ammonia. It gave me a head rush and felt way too strong for the nostrils. Then, it kicked in, and my ears were pulsating as well as my heartbeats, starting to pound at a millionth of a second. It had some kind of overall effect and a feeling of euphoria.

"Strong little crap!" I said as Tae looked at my expression with an evil smile and giggled one more time. "What is this shit?"

She replied, hiding her face behind her bangs, "Poppers!" She said it is very popular nowadays.

"What the hell?" I thought.

The recreational drug didn't last but a minute. It was not worth my time.

She kept sniffing it and shared it with Mackenzie and Colton. They seemed to love it.

I looked around at the dance floor, and it seemed as if everyone was hooked doing poppers. It seemed as if I was the only one who didn't know what that was. People in the crowd sniffed their own poppers. I guess I wasn't as wild as I thought I was after all.

I turned to Colton. His eyes were completely dark and not the blue I had remembered. Perhaps his pupils had dilated for whatever he was doing with MacKenzie. He scared the wits out of me for a moment, but I blamed it on the poor lightning and the heat of the moment. At first, I kind of saw him as if he were in another realm, but I guess my mind was playing tricks on me. Colton was motionless as well as Mackenzie. They appeared to be in midair, and the rest of the crowd started to move slowly. Go figure. I blamed it on the popper's reaction.

For a moment, I had to go to the restroom, and as I was standing in line, I kept staring back at the dance floor. This sordid music was rushing through my head. I immediately thought that my vision was playing tricks on me. At one point, I doubted the reality I was in. My sight and body emotions were totally two alien worlds, one had nothing to do with the other. I was about to lose it. I blamed it on "that thing"—the darn poppers, darn it!

"I am not trying that crap any longer; that's not for me,"
I kept saying to myself.

Then, I was pushed by a skinny, hairy dude who was
upset and tried to pick a fight, "Hey, dude, go; come on!"

Somehow, I was holding back the line to the men's room
and was kind of lost for a second, but his intrusion brought
me back to the reality of that moment.

"Sorry, dude!" I politely excused myself scratching my
head.

The guy looked at me menacingly.

I was still so annoyed by it. I wondered about the whole
thing, but I had no time to stop and think about it. I just let it
go; I kept thinking that I'd figure it out later.

Once out of the restroom area, I walked back to the dance
floor. I made my move quickly. I knew Tae already dug me,
and we started kissing again. I felt privileged. We were right
up against the wall and excited when Mackenzie showed up
and called her. Damn, she spoiled the moment. Tae
apologized and left me standing there.

"See ya' in a bit," was the last thing she said to me.

I kept dancing on my own and followed them with my
eyes. The girls joined Nico, and I guess they split together.
Yet, a minute later, I was dancing with Mackenzie. I didn't
see, Nico, Tae or Colton.

I was confused and thought, "What the heck?"

Mackenzie moved her awesome body as if she had a
couple of seductive spirits inside of her, and I thought that
was hilarious. Moments later, I don't remember anything
else; it is all a void in my head.

***

Next thing I recalled—I was on the road again driving
my car despite the fact that I liked to sit around and let
alcohol wear off so I wouldn't get into an accident. I've done
this religiously every time I party in Hollywood before I

151

drive. How is it, then, that Colton was right by my side as if I had imagined it all? It was as if we had never gotten out of the car, met the girls, kissed the girls, or danced and drank with them. How weird was that?

The top on my convertible was down, and the radio was blasting a wild song I liked so much back then by Twisted Sisters, a song called "Not Gonna Take It." Colton was singing aloud. At that point, I was confused and wondering whatever was wrong with this picture? Colton kept smiling and tapping his left palm on his knees, and I sang along out loud, too, just like him and got into the euphoria of the moment.

When we passed the San Fernando Valley, he said, "Carlo, turn here."

I immediately felt that I had fallen into some kind of a trance; I couldn't make any decisions on my own, more now than before, so I kept driving.

We went in the direction of the canyons, and then he said, "Turn right there."

I wanted to complain or say something, but I didn't have the will to do so. That was so odd when he said, "Stop right here."

I did, and we were in the middle of nowhere. A few lights flashed around us, but I don't remember other vehicles there. It was mostly dark and empty.

Colton looked around and said to me, "Go now!"

And off I went. For some unknown reason, I felt under his mind control. I had no say or will with regards to that. Call it a robotic state or something freaky like that.

In my teen years, I came to LA and knew this huge city by heart. As much as I wanted to get away from the Hollywood area at first, somehow I kept running around in circles, unlike me. I usually settled in Florentine Gardens and joined the regulars. Meeting Colton was no accident. I knew something was happening to me because I had never acted this way before.

I looked at the time and it was 2:30 AM already. I thought to stop and drop Colton off just anywhere. I was stressed out and kind of pissed. I still had another hour to make it to my mom's home all the way to Long Beach. I lived in Ventura County then but had promised to visit her the next morning. Topanga Canyon was a long ways from my mom's, and I was getting tired. My eyes felt heavy. The alcohol was gone from my system, It was not fun anymore, and I wasn't so happy.

Colton noticed it and said, "We're almost done, dude. Please be patient for a few more minutes, okay?!"

He waved his hand over my forehead and that made me feel totally relaxed and willing to follow directions against my own reasoning. Colton had something like an illuminated artifact, so to speak, attached to the palm of his hand.

We then stopped the car. He got out. I felt I was going into a trance again, then this odd void feeling, and then we were back on the road again.

***

"Okay, this guy had some kind of power over me," I thought to myself.

He ordered me to drive back to Hollywood Hills.

I drove against my will, but I just couldn't say, "No." I was a bit uptight already.

The gas tank light lit up and showed that we were running pretty low.

I guess that Colton read my mind, and he said not to worry about that as he pointed at the light. He mentioned something like gas was not going to run out. He put his eyes back on the road and kept staring at his watch. I obeyed although I had a negative feeling about it. I was not sure what to think anymore and felt that Colton was already abusing his privileges. I felt like I was being used for his demands, but I had no control of my guts to tell him off.

We went uphill, found Beachwood Street, and stopped by a beautiful house with a great view of the whole city of Hollywood. Colton, or whatever his name was, got out again. I began to doubt Colton was his real name. I was frightened he could be a criminal and that I was his unwilling accomplice. I began to fear for my life as well, even if I felt no threats from him, yet I realized he was a total stranger to me.

He took a big breath and said calmly, "Do not go anywhere; stay put. I'll be back soon, dude!"

His eyes turned black totally, and it freaked me out. My whole spine stood up on end, and the last of my hairs on my back as well.

He had turned into some kind of a demon like in those low-budget horror films. I began to sweat on my hands and forehead. I felt strong heartbeats in my chest, as if I had jogged uphill for a mile.

Dogs barked from someone's backyard nearby, and then the barks turned into weak howling.

I stayed in the car as Colton had demanded of me. So, I decided to play my music to kill the eerie mood of the moment. Colton's game had turned very peculiar indeed. I didn't dare move a finger, and to this day, I still don't know how he pulled it off. I haven't figured it out.

I assumed my position as told. I began to feel restless; my arms and legs got heavy and numb. I couldn't believe that I was stationed there inside the vehicle for at least, what? Until 3:30 AM?

"That's impossible, not long ago it was 2:30 AM ... what the ...?"

But before I could complain or realize something very fishy was going on, I heard footsteps on the concrete sidewalk.

"Thank God," I thought.

My brain recognized the sound of his *Florsheim Duke Side Zip Boots.*

The Unlikely Hitchhiker

I saw the unlikely hitchhiker rushing towards my car through the rear view mirror. He seemed picture perfect and very human with his relaxed, loose, long hairstyle and a nice impeccable leather jacket, yet he felt like another reality to me—perhaps less of a human or something other than a human. He seemed to me like the hero of an epic movie with the mix of a suspenseful and psychological thriller like an old Hitchcock classic.

Colton got in my car and handled a small device similar to a small cell phone. Back in the 1980s we had the big bulky and heavy dinosaur sort of car phones attached to a wired box. What he had was an object that resembled a modern iPhone, something like a hundred years in the future. That's exactly how that thing looked to me. I had the feeling that it was a communicator of some kind.

Before he said anything to me, I saw unusual lights flickering inside a house; it was the house he had stepped out from.

He smiled, and his blue eyes sparkled again. He patted me on the back of my right shoulder.

"Let's go, man!" he said smiling.

I decompressed and felt free to move around without feeling that I was trapped any longer. I didn't even blink anymore. I felt disoriented and allied to his orders.

He pressed the screen on his tiny device, and something began to move inside—a video of sorts. He didn't let me or want me to see clearly. He kept the thing away from my view, but I still heard sounds.

Back on the road and going up and down the hills, I drove expecting directions from Colton. He kept looking at the electronic device on his hand, and once again, he told me to follow another direction, which turned into a serpentine-like road. I remember I read a street sign, Durand Drive. It was very quiet and not so illuminated. We ended up in a darker spot.

Then, a tiny European car made contact with us. It flickered its low lights on us.

Colton asked me to slow down to meet where the toy car had stopped, and I did.

The passenger window went down smoothly, and Colton told me to open my window as well. A male hand reached out, and I was told to do the same. My hand trembled. The sketchy figure inside was a tall man with fuzzy blue hair; he looked funny cramped inside such a tiny car. He handed me a package without saying a word. Colton handed me a cold glass capsule filled with a weightless liquid of sorts.

I prayed again not to be involved in any illicit practice like illegal drugs or something that could land me behind bars. The funny thing was that I felt as if I were possessed by some sort of invisible force. I thought that, if I got arrested at that very moment, the cops would not believe my story. As a Catholic, I pleaded to all the saints in Heaven to help me out of this situation or at least let me off the hook quickly.

The more I tried to remember the stranger's features, the more I couldn't recall them. I saw some glimpses of him, but I cannot remember many details except his long, very white arm sticking out of the blue-and-white, tiny car. I was told to keep on driving again in the same direction, which ended around the Hollywood reservoir lake.

We made another stop where a very skinny guy was jogging. Colton got out of my car, and they met to exchange just a few words. I looked through the rear-view mirror when I caught just a glimpse of the mysterious jogger vanishing in the dark. Colton hurried back. At that time, he looked a little more than worried and asked me to drive faster. We turned and took Mulholland Drive, which overlooks the city of Hollywood at an angle.

I was attentive to his orders. I tried to keep in mind that I was not acting spontaneously and was being victimized by this creep Colton who was not fun anymore. He had become a kidnapper, but there was no way I could prove that.

The Unlikely Hitchhiker

The last I remember was that he told me to stop suddenly again. Then, he got out of the car and got into a telephone booth. He probably made a call. I don't know; I was not interested anymore. He came back with a million-dollar smile slapped on his manly-looking face and told me to get back on the freeway.

We drove back onto the 101 Northbound towards the valley again. I lost any sense of direction. My thoughts were intervened, and my free will was held captive under his commands.

My mind kept thinking, "What a mess I've got myself into!"

We drove by some areas where I actually saw Colton's body start to glitch and dematerialize right in front of me. The whole thing was frightening to me: teeth, lips, facial features, nose, clothing, shoes, etc. He had turned into a nightmare, my nightmare.

Is it possible that I was dreaming this whole thing? No dream in history could last this long, and no dream of mine had a beginning, middle and end. I wanted it to be over already, but everything had turned into one of those thrilling roller coaster rides at Six Flags Magic Mountain.

Even Colton's behavior had become very odd. The worst part was the control he still had over me. He did not realize that I was able to begin to control what and how I felt, but ironically, I was the one who wanted to go all the way to the end. I was now very alarmed but curious. With this much weirdness and way too much mystery, I wanted to get to the end of it. I started to pay very close attention to what was going on because I finally had total control of myself, but I avoided any thoughts that could get in the way. Colton might be able to still read me.

When I was young, back in my twenties, I was usually the kind of guy with a strong personality, hardheaded in a way, but very talented with just about anyone in general. Humans always captivated me; they think that they can hide who they are and pose as someone else. With that said, I was still very easy and pleasant when I felt that they tried to diminish or impress me in anyway. I used to be good at reading people's minds. I did not respond well when anyone demanded anything of me, or when others talked rough to me. I tended to retaliate with intelligence, either desist cooperating, or put up a fight, yet with Colton none of that was happening. So, I knew I was not being myself that night. I was acting very drugged for that matter. I thought of that over and over until I calmed myself to conserve my mental sanity. Perhaps that is what freed me from his total control over me.

Colton's image stopped malfunctioning; his whole person was solid all over again. He bent to his feet and proceeded to take his shoes off, turned to the back seat, and retrieved a backpack.

"When in God's name did he put that backpack inside my car?" I thought. I couldn't remember that he ever did and without me noticing that before.

He pulled a pair of heavy hiking boots from the backpack, replaced them with his nice shoes while taking a deep breath.

I definitely was not all there. How in the world would I remember some things? Other things were just a surprise to me as if I had been turned on or off and then found out that a lot had escaped my mind.

Out of the corner of my eye, I noticed Colton pull out what appeared to be a rare material from the same bag. I turned to see what it was. It was a pair of baby blue socks made of the finest silk I had ever seen in my whole life. Yet, once placed on his feet, they appeared to be made of a tough material. In other words, they changed shape. They turned into the kind of socks used for hiking. I expected his boots to stink like hell for they looked overworked and dirty, but they didn't have a smell at all.

At that point, what caught my attention about Colton was his pale hands and skin, like the bloodless body of a dead human or perhaps more like synthetic skin.

"Ohh, sweet Jesus!"

Everything was turning bizarre by the minute, and my emotions were irrelevant. I was involved in who knows what and there was no way out until the whole adventure was over. All I prayed was to keep my mind together and not show the guy that I was free from his control. Would I be able to pull that off? I didn't know that, but I was going to push it to the end and solve the mystery around the man.

This dude's nails and fingers were more purplish than the usual pink like that of human's hands. I remember that he never asked my opinion about anything, but he kept getting me involved in his spoken comments. I can say that he was nice to me in that way. He kept smiling to himself. I did not question or try to make any sense of all that because I didn't want him to do anything to control me again.

I had the feeling that I was going to wake up from a nightmare or perhaps someone was playing a joke on me, but, hey, it had gone way too far. I felt I had to recollect my thoughts, my mind, my whatever. I had to be myself again.

Colton also proceeded to take his jacket off. I observed that his jeans had dried mud spots in a few areas. He decided to show me his cowboy silver buckle. I had no interest in hearing the story of how he got it nor have any sort of conversation with him. On the other hand, I was definitely sick of driving up and down without any say, and now I had to fake it to the end. Now that I think about it, maybe he was testing me to see if I was still under his control. I kept putting on a show, like if I was still in the same state of mind as before.

The story about how he got the buckle was that he had met a famous actor, now deceased, in one of the wealthiest neighborhoods of the Los Angeles area called Bel Air, where a lot of people from the motion picture industry resided.

"The Duke" was a famous actor whom at the time I didn't know or care to know about because of the situation. There were many dukes, but "The Duke" he talked about was the famous John Wayne who had died just a few days after I arrived in the USA in the year 1979. Of course, I didn't ask anything about it.

The only odd thing to me was when Colton said, "Oh, you'll get the chance to meet him one day, you'll see."

That was when I realized he was deceased and I was very much alive, so I thought. That made me shiver a little, but I tried to stay in control of my own emotions. I just wanted him to get it over with.

He then told me that he was going to do some hiking, and that I was welcome to join him, but I had no desire whatsoever to bounce around with him. He stared at me for a moment, like if it were up to me to make a decision. I thought that he was testing me again. I kept thinking that he was checking for a sign in my body language, or my facial expressions. I think everything pointed in that direction.

He smiled and said, "Suit yourself, dude."

I didn't even blink once and kept my face with a stone-cold expression.

Then, the impossible happened.

He murmured into my ear, "Courage is being scared to death but saddling up anyway."

I don't know what button he pressed inside of me, but I knew I was on a mission with this guy. I had a duty to fulfill and that was to participate in a plan with a total stranger who appeared in my inner thoughts as if I had always known him. I couldn't help but laugh as we did in the very beginning when we met.

Then, we parked in the middle of nowhere again. I have no idea where I was.

"Give me hell, yeah!" he yelled and slapped my hand. "Dude, get your hiking boots and put them on!" said Colton as he rushed to the back of the trunk of my car.

He pointed with his finger and had a joker's smile on his face.

Indeed, I did have a pair of hiking boots and clothes in there; I usually kept hiking gear because I enjoyed doing some hiking myself back then. So, I did follow his instructions and got ready.

We hiked uphill by many twists and turns; the roads were kind of dark regardless of some traffic flashing their lights as they drove by. We got deeper into a desolated area. Colton was still playing with his little device that sounded like an electronic toy. Regardless of all the action, I was still interested in getting rid of the hitchhiker from hell or at least uncover his mystery.

We arrived at a construction site, and from a distance, I noticed yellow lights that would guide us up the unmarked road. I tried to record all of that in detail in my head, so I wouldn't forget for whatever that was worth. We slowed down because we looked up to the dark skies and saw some spot lights. At first, I thought they were those spot lights to advertise an event, yet they were very strange lights. Their brightness illuminated the whole hill like a wildfire. When I turned my face towards him, I saw a huge, silver blunt instrument that was sticking out of his left boot and under the leg of his jeans as if he had concealed it for some reason. I didn't know what to think; it was either a gun or a knife. I didn't know what, but my intuition played with me, and I started sweating bullets. I thought he was guiding me to a place where he could easily kill or dismember me. There were many crazies out there, and my mind was racing with many distorted thoughts.

Not knowing anything was to my advantage. I could do something to defend myself when the right time came. He started a conversation again, and he was very bold with me.

"I hope you are not freaking out on me," he said.

I nodded and tried to pretend everything was just like in the beginning; I did not complain anymore. The thought that perhaps he had slipped a drug into my drink or something back at Gino's II came back into my head, but after a while I realized that everything at that place and time had to do with other forces, those I hadn't experienced before, not at that level. I tried to look and sound very calm.

"No man, what are you talking about?" I said naturally.

He blew some air with his mouth and said, "You know that you are a very special dude!"

"Right!" I said without any expression.

He looked like he was trying to read me.

"I guess so!" he said as he gazed at the black night full of stars. "Let's crash here for a few minutes."

I wondered about that because I thought the one who should be asking for a break would be me and not him, so I sat on a huge rock and looked around. I wasn't scared anymore.

All I remember at that moment was that Colton had that crystal thingy hidden in his boots and showed it to me. It was exactly like the one I remember now from the movie "Men in Black." Then my whole memory was gone again, a total void. I was still awake, and thoughts were rushing into my head until we were back in my car, and I was driving again without any recollection of how I got from point A to point B.

We were cruising the serpentine roads again and away from that area. Colton asked me to roll down the window to breathe some air. I don't remember when I put the top up, but what I do remember was that he called me by my name, and I was under his control one more time and hated it. True, I needed some air. It was kind of chilly, but I liked it. Colton's hair was all over his face when I noticed a strange mark on his neck. I couldn't make out if that was some kind of symbol, a tattoo, or what in God's name. I had to concentrate on the road; the traffic turned from constantly busy into almost no traffic at all. Once again, I got tired of his presence; it was all about him having absolute control over me.

Out of the blue he said, "Dude, I need you to come with me this time and meet me halfway. I need you to help me with something that I can't do on my own, and I promise you that I will let you off the hook soon."

He blinked his sparkling blue eyes again giving me the thumbs up.

I looked away because I had had it. I couldn't take it anymore, and he knew it.

"Do I have any choice?" I asked myself.

I guess that my anger and frowns were enough for Colton to realize that I had had enough of him. I'm positive that he noticed and read it all over my face. He became apologetic and reasonable, explaining to me in a few words that there was a reason behind it. He added that I didn't understand at that moment in time but that one day I would be told that I had a mission to accomplish and that I was all right with it. Everything would be very clear to me then. Colton assured me that I would always be of use to them.

I just wanted all of it to be over with!

He then said, "Okay, dude, you have only two choices here." He counted with his fingers. "One, either you help me out now."

He looked around and up to the sky as if he were trying to hide from something.

"We need to complete this mission together, and I promise that you will be free to go home."

My face was unchangeable.

He said it over and over and going around in circles.

"Or, you don't move a finger, but then you'll need to wait up for me, and I may take a few hours of your time."

He paused for a long moment. Took a deep breath.

Colton smiled and said, "Maybe a day or two and it won't be fair to you. You seem very tired, dude. I think that you are more than ready to go home. You don't want to be here any longer, right?"

"Right," I replied.

Obviously, my answer was a positive yes to help him out. Did I have a choice? Of course not!

I looked at my gas gauge and the needle showed a full tank.

"What the hell! Not again! When did that happen?"

I kind of remembered that we stopped at a gas station before driving back into the hills but can't recall how in the world we filled the tank. Pieces and bits of info started to flood my mind, and I remember that Colton had asked me to stop in the middle of nowhere. He got out of the car and filled up the tank. I don't recall seeing anyone, human that is, or seeing him pay for gas, or if he paid for gas at all.

I said nothing.

"I need you to turn your emergency lights on as soon as you can stop the car on the right side of the road near that hill!" he said abruptly.

He pointed out to a very dark spot. I moved over on the two-way road to the shoulder quickly but steadily. I slowed down making a complete stop next to what looked like a black wall.

We spent a few minutes there.

He gave me another toy like the one he held in his hands and said, "If you see any cops or run into an emergency and I'm not back yet, press the bluish button, OK?" He gave me the serious look and continued saying, "If a yellow light starts blinking, press it down for three seconds, OK?"

His look meant business, and I knew that was very important for the mission, but also for my own safety. Then, Colton was gone.

He was back in no time and in the car again. He returned with the smell of a peculiar odor like that of a computer in use. I didn't know. After that, he told me to keep driving straight up, turn back towards the San Fernando Valley area, and then follow the road to Tujunga Canyon Road where you can barely see a light at night.

We parked.

I thought again about my fate. Colton had something in his boots that made me nervous, and he didn't look friendly anymore. I was determined that I had to survive. It didn't matter what it took, but I had to make it for me and my family. I got out cautiously. He asked me to follow him. I could have run back to the car and driven off, but I wasn't sure if that thing in his boot was a gun. I had to play my cards wisely.

We walked in the dark for a few minutes. There were a lot of loose small rocks and sand. Sometimes I kind of slid but kept a firm step, so I wouldn't fall on my butt.

The time had come when he pulled that thing out of his boot. It was a shiny bright object like a platinum bar. It was long and had a protuberance; it did look soft to the touch. He parted in a new direction in the middle of nowhere while I was looking away and noticed a wild animal staring. Perhaps it was a mountain lion or a coyote. I don't know, but the animal freaked out on his own and ran off.

Not long after, I thought I saw something like a wild hare in the distance. I caught sight of a wired fence with really high gates. I was shocked that it appeared out of nowhere.

Colton smiled and said, "Follow me, dude."

He looked up again. A bright light shined down from above near a spot up ahead.

We walked side by side toward it.

There was a heavy chain with a big thing that looked like a padlock in the middle of the gates. On top of the tall fence, there was some barbed wire around the area of contact.

I started to get anxious.

"Oh, my God, oh, my God," I kept whispering to myself.

There was a small building all the way in the back—a warehouse located inside the fenced area.

Colton unlocked the gates without a key, and then he locked them back up.

I complained, "Hey, dude, why are you locking that thing up? We won't have a chance to run and get out if this thing blows."

The truth was that I was scared to death. Everything was so unreal.

Colton replied very calmly, "For safety." He blinked once and kept walking.

I found a strange-looking rock and picked it up. I slid it inside the pocket of my jacket hoping to keep it; I like to collect strange things sometimes.

We then walked for a total of thirty steps maybe from the main gate. We went around the back of the building, and there was a small door that looked like a service window as in a drive-thru-fast-food place. It seemed to be made out of strong metal. Colton pressed on a latch, and the metal thing opened up. He got in and told me to keep close to him and touch nothing. I did. It was extremely tight and slim. Luckily, I was in great shape and that helped me to get by without a lot of effort.

Once inside the concrete walls, we found an empty square room. What bothered me was that it was getting very cold, and I started to shiver. Colton pulled out his fancy digital thingy and pressed more buttons. Some sounds were released. To my surprise, the whole building glitched, and I could see up to the sky. Then, the whole building trembled like a small earthquake, and there was this light on top coming from a dark cloud. My lips trembled more now because he didn't say anything at all about what just happened. Actually, my whole body began to tremble, but I was already way too compromised to run the hell out.

"This is nothing more than child's play!" he said and told me to place the instrument closer to my eyes. "Are you ready?" he asked.

166

I doubt he wanted me to do anything at all. In my head I kept saying, "Ready for what?" But I promised to keep my thoughts to myself, so I let out a, "Yep," with a cynical smile on my face.

Colton put his backpack on the floor and walked towards me. He told me to take my jacket and my shirt off.

"Okay," I said without resisting.

At the same time, he was doing that, too.

It was now so cold that I shivered a lot more than before.

"Go stand there by that wall!"

He guided me next to a short tunnel.

"Where?" I asked, not because I didn't know where to go, but because I was trying to see whatever else I needed to see. Damn, it was too dark for me to even guess what it was.

He pointed at a fluorescent orange circle on the floor. There was no way I could miss it, and I moved to stand right inside it. Colton did the same in another orange circle. He took his jacket and shirt and threw it away from the area.

"What?" I screamed in my head.

His stuff dematerialized while mine was still on the ground.

As he stood inside the other fluorescent orange circle, he used the device.

"When this is over, you may go," he prompted.

"How would I know?" I questioned him.

He smiled; his blue eyes sparkled brighter this time.

"You'll know. Trust me," he added.

A long minute passed.

I felt this energy hitting my chest and warming up the whole place to a pleasant temperature. The sound was more sordid and stopped soon enough.

"Arrivederci, Italiano dude!" he cynically yelled, smiling at me.

The lights and Colton were gone like a magic trick in the blink of an eye!

"What the hell?" I couldn't resist to curse one more time.

Then, I quickly picked up my clothes and put them back on. I ran the hell out of there as quickly as I could. It was my chance to escape from that mad abduction, the strangest one I've ever had.

When I looked back, the whole place had vanished and crumbled into crystal sand, which melted into the ground like smoke. Everything there disappeared right before my eyes.

I resumed running without looking back. I tripped and stumbled on the dust and rocks and finally made it to my precious car. I felt free and released from all that mental pressure around Colton.

The emergency lights on my car were still blinking. The road was completely quiet and desolated, as expected. I could see the sun on the horizon piercing through a few grayish clouds. I drove off like a maniac.

I was so tired but still had to drive to my mom's, who lived in Long Beach. So, I stopped for some coffee and doughnuts on the way to give my body and mind a chance to fully wake up. I was hungry, anxious, and desperate. I couldn't go back to my mom's in this condition. I'd be questioned, and I wasn't about to tell all. I couldn't help it. I knew I was still acting strange and suspicious about something important. I had to calm down, or else I had to explain my weird behavior. I had to get back to my old self but that was going to take some time.

I drove around the same streets in Hollywood as I had done the previous night with the hitchhiker aboard. I wanted to make sure I wasn't hallucinating. The tangible proof was all I had as my only truth.

My mind was rolling with many emotions. I remembered about the rock in my pocket, so I stuck my hand in my pocket, and what I pulled out was totally absurd. I stopped my car on the side of the road to have a better look. The rock had turned into sand. I got out and poured the sand all over the dirt just to confirm the validity of my experience. The sand turned into little crystals that vaporized when it hit the ground right before my eyes, leaving me speechless.

I heard someone say, "Hey dude, what's up?"

I looked everywhere and then realized it was Colton's voice!

***

After all these years, my take on Colton is that I was not chosen randomly. Colton was or is someone whom I've met previously, but I have no recollection of that because for some reason my mind can't pinpoint the motives. Remember that experiencers are not crazy lunatics even if the world judges them like that. We always have a plan, or we're part of a plan.

That being said, Colton did call me by my name. He knew it, and once he called me, I was under some sort of a spell! During my adventure with this character, I kept asking myself why would I let him tell me what to do! But I knew I had to follow his lead and that's what I did.

I also believe he was some sort of a secret agent like James Bond but who, instead, traveled through time and space to fix things in our world like technicians do. He completed his mission, and the reason I was in it was because people like me have hidden codes that agents like Colton need to use for things they'll need to eventually accomplish their missions. I did have the impression that he might have been some sort of synthetic humanoid with an artificial intelligence. When his eyes turned black, it was as if they had a liquid that triggered his emotions.

His motive about going from one party to the next was not to have fun but, in the first case at the Florentine Gardens, was to meet me there to pair me up with him! I was or had a key he needed! During the next party at Gino's II, I'm positive that the heavy-set guy with the two hot girls had a plan that also aided Colton. Then, all the strange stops we made on that wild goose chase, including meeting up with that weird guy in the tiny car, all served as steps to getting Colton to the warehouse on time for a lift off to wherever he came from.

Perhaps Colton had enemies that were tailing him, and I was his Earth-bound cover during all these secret rendezvous. Perhaps he was a benevolent being, as he closely resembled the Nordics with his blond, blue-eyed appearance. Perhaps, therefore, he was a Pleiadian on a secret mission on Earth to help humans somehow. I will never know for sure. Although he did say that I would eventually find out all about him, it hasn't happened to this day, more than thirty years later. These are the kinds of haunting mysteries that experiencers like me have to live with our whole lives without knowing the true answers.

13.

Mr. Moretti's Cult

"I immediately felt the presence of two spirits.
The entities wanted to enter my flesh!"

"How are you doin', son?"

Sometime back in 2005, one of my customers greeted me at the convenience store where I worked for many years as a general manager in Miami, Florida. The friendly voice was accompanied by a light tap on my shoulder. That day of the week I was busy restocking merchandise. Still, I turned around with a smile to greet whomever that person was. I knew my regulars mostly for the way they smelled, walked or talked, and that particular customer was no stranger to me. I knew that Habanero cigar smell from a mile away, so to speak.

"Hey, Mr. Moretti, I'm doing just fine. How are you, sir?"

The handsome, old man wearing a white guayavera shirt got closer to me and said almost whispering, "I know about those spirits that are tormenting you, son. Don't let them scare you!"

My smile soon disappeared. That was so unexpected that I didn't know what to make of it at first because Mr. Moretti was sort of a joker sometimes. But the truth was, during that week, I was having some otherworldly experiences and had only told one person about my spiritual struggle, my personal assistant Vicky.

Victoria Molina was someone who had gained my total respect and confidence over the years. She was right there also restocking inside the cashier's booth. I saw her from behind the glass, and she had a look of wonder about my unusual facial expression. I thought for a moment that she had deceived me. Although my assistant, she seemed puzzled just like me. I refused to believe that Vicky had anything to do with my client's unusual and strange comment.

Clearing my throat quite a bit, I said to the old gentleman, "Why do you say such a thing, Mr. Moretti?"

There was this penetrating odor coming from him like weeds regardless of his neat appearance. I couldn't guess what it was or where the upsetting odor was coming from. Maybe it came out of his clothes or perhaps from his skin. I thought that was odd; I've been around him before and I never noticed it.

He had the audacity to continue talking about the subject as he kept chewing on his cigar. "I have some friendly spirit guides that are my friends, and they told me all about you. They wanna help you!"

I was not really upset, but I was bothered by his persistence. Customers were coming in and out and walking around us. I didn't want them to judge me as a lunatic or a crazy person. His comments had become kind of embarrassing already.

"Who knows all about me, and they wanna help me to do what?" I confronted him in a very low voice, hoping not to hurt his feelings.

He quickly replied, "To strengthen your spiritual abilities, son."

Mr. Moretti was probably in his late 70s, and I did not feel threatened at any time, yet it was definitely an unwanted burden to me at that moment in my life. Although he'd been a customer at my store for many years, we never had the chance to engage in any small talk, not even before that day. All I recalled ever saying to him was, "Good day," "Thank you for your business," or "Goodbye." Previously, I'd seen him in my security cameras talking to Vicky. But their conversation was limited to simple weather conditions or his old, beloved Cuba.

On that specific day, minutes before he showed up, I had a talk with my assistant about some boring marketing strategies the corporation needed us to do. So, I decided to help her put away merchandise on the floor because our extra help had called in sick. That is how I believe Mr. Moretti and I had this weird encounter. Vicky once had mentioned Mr. Moretti's unusual talk, but since she was a Catholic, she didn't want to listen to what, in her words, were nothing less than a Santeria cult kind of talk. I always laughed about her deductions. Soon enough, Vicky interrupted the fanatical old man and came to my rescue. She knew I wanted to get away but didn't want to be rude to my customers, in particular that nice old man who probably wanted to talk to anyone because maybe he felt lonely. Who knows what went on in his mind? She distracted the old man, tried to get him away from me, and did. The old-timer held his breath. I felt that he knew what Vicky's intentions were.

"Vicky, I'll talk to you later, OK?" he said it without even looking at her.

He never took his eyes off me. I felt his hand on my shoulder on his way out. At that point, I had had enough of him, but that was his way of letting me know that our conversation wasn't over.

As he went out the door, he whispered to me in gasping tones, "I need to speak to you privately, boy. You hear?"

I caught a smile on his wrinkled, pale face, and my heart pounded with fear for a few seconds. I nodded so he'd leave me alone.

My reasoning about him was that he was a nutcase, though he intrigued me, and he was right about my restless nights after all. He pumped gas into his well-kept 1970's El Camino and drove off while talking to himself.

Sometimes I enjoyed having a good laugh about all the unbelievable stuff that happened to me since I can remember. Other times, paranormal activities like my endless nightmares continued on with a different chapter every night reliving the same story. How strange was that for thrills and chills leading my pitiful life? That was totally crazy, but it was my own reality.

I questioned Vicky about the whole incident, and she was as astonished as I was. She swore that she never had a conversation about me in that regards with the old man, but that he always asked for me every time he came into the store, as if he had wanted to have a one-on-one conversation with me.

The next time Mr. Moretti showed up, he came straight at me and said, "Good morning, young man."

I thanked him for calling me a young man; I was in my mid-40s already.

"We need to talk now," he said.

I smiled at him and replied, "Follow me, sir!"

We walked back towards my office because I was embarrassed others might hear our strange talk. I felt as if I was under a spell by an experienced mentalist. I saw Vicky over at the counter, and she had a wondering look on her face, perhaps puzzled about my meeting with the old Cuban man. I gestured back to her with my "It's okay" expression in response.

Once in my office, I offered Mr. Moretti a cup of our fresh-brewed coffee. He wasn't that thrilled about it; rather, he mumbled about Cuban coffee being the best in the world. Then he said something funny about our security cameras, where I can spy on my customers and employees. The old man was all over the place with his conversation before he landed with what he wanted to talk to me about.

"I have always seen you around physically and spiritually, you know."

He started by making strange small talk. I limited myself by just nodding.

"I knew from the very beginning about your abilities."

He paused and looked at me.

"I'm a healer, you know? Like a medicine doctor, I deal with it at a spiritual level, you know. I help clean evil spirits from people like you and also can heal physical pain."

I hummed very quietly for a few seconds and wondered about all his weirdness; I was afraid that everything he said made perfect sense to me, regardless of my poor opinion about his reality.

"What do you mean, Mr. Moretti?" I said because it's hard to believe what you always knew in the back of your mind. However, I smiled and tried to keep a straight face because all of it was crazy and funny at the same time. I looked away and tried to stay focused to show him all the respect he deserved. I kind of kept quiet and let him continue.

"I came today with a mission and that is to help you out, but you need to willingly accept my help."

I felt kind of queasy, as if I were about to make a pact with the devil himself. That was an awful feeling. He sounded so preposterous that I was willing to accept whatever he proposed to me just for the hell of it and get him off my back.

"How's your neck doing?" he said, moving his finger as he pointed to my neck.

I took a second look at him. I had just pulled a muscle a few nights before and was going through this excruciating pain. I was taking pain killers and had not said anything to anyone about that yet, so his observation came a little more of a surprise to me.

Deep inside of me, I did not know what to make of this man claiming these psychic abilities, a ridiculous circus sideshow to me. Yet, the old man was dead serious about these things that were very real in my personal life. I was trying to put them behind because they did not make any sense to me. How could that be possible? How did he know I was experiencing these spiritual battles on a daily basis? Even though I was becoming very skeptical about them, he was reconfirming that my nightmares were very real. I was blaming everything to a mental disorder, and this man was confirming I wasn't insane. It was really happening, and now I was truly puzzled.

Every single night in my sleep, I was literally attacked by unknown dark and evil entities. I had many accounts with the paranormal and had my full share of unpleasant experiences with negative entities. How can you fight what you can't see? They confronted me, sometimes as if their mission was to subdue me or just have some form of communication with me.

I was going nuts. It had been going on for years.

I felt like sound waves were tuning in with my brain and showing me visions that would appear and disappear in a matter of seconds. Even if I were in a dark room, the whole event would light up right there sometimes giving me the impression I was in the middle of the whole commotion. I called it a "vivid vision." It was becoming very stressful to me, indeed. Sometimes I felt drained and lost every morning because of it.

"How could I go on like this?" I thought.

I became sad and turned very skeptical about my experiences. Wherever I turned, I've read, learned, or had people advise me that it was my own mind producing these delusions that could be psychologically or medically explained as schizophrenia or hallucinations. I did understand that diagnosis; it was very loud and clear to me in my head. The point was that these "issues" never stopped, and the more I denied it, the more they became stronger and more vivid.

At times, I was tired of all the nonsense around me. I was tired of my life naturally tapping into the unknown. Nothing at all was helping me to achieve a better life in tune with my whole world. Instead, I became short-tempered and bitter. Most of the time, I couldn't care less what those around me thought about me. What I wanted was to have the certainty that everything was the real deal and not something produced by a figment of my imagination.

That day in my office concluded with Mr. Moretti asking me if I would allow him to send me a couple of spirits to help me out with my issues. I was desperate and accepted what he had to offer without giving it another thought. However, I still considered that whatever he said to me that morning was nothing but a bunch of bologna. Still, Mr. Moretti left my place all happy.

Vicky wondered what went on with the old man in my office.

"What was that all about?" she asked me all worried.

I laughed, "Woman, let me ask you, but be honest with me!"

"What is it?" she asked me with a funny smirk on her face.

We both looked at the old Cuban man biting down on his fat Cuban cigar as he drove off and vanished in the traffic.

I turned to the Vicky and complained, "Are you sure you had not talked to the old man about me in any way at all?"

Her facial color turned pale at the question.

"Absolutely not!" she responded.

I believed her. I've known Vicky for at least five years; we've been working together for that long. I know that she was the kind of person who knew how to keep things private, but the old man was so beguiling that I had to doubt her for a moment until I organized my thoughts.

"Well, I'll tell you what went on in my office with that weirdo." I told her everything; she listened carefully without any interruptions.

She then told me that she wasn't surprised at all because she suspected that he practiced Santeria or white magic. She couldn't believe I accepted his proposal. Vicky warned me I was playing with fire. But I had little Christian faith then, so by the old man trying to be nice to me and send me a couple of spirits to my home was either a laughing matter or could also be a solution to my nightmares. Who knows? I was willing to risk it.

"Hey Vicky, don't worry about it. The spirits won't know where I live," I chuckled. "I never gave the old man my address."

I thought it was hilarious to see how she fearfully replied.

"I would never dare to accept anything that comes from that man, you know," she said. "I'm afraid he's into witchery for real."

I thought Vicky was making a big deal about the whole thing and was getting paranoid for something that to me was kind of really stupid and insignificant.

"If I believed in his nonsense one hundred percent, then I'd be frightened myself, don't you think?" I added.

Still, she warned me to be careful.

I thought about the pain in my neck. Suddenly, it had disappeared after he left. The old man probably did it when he tapped me on my shoulder casually.

"Hey, I have to admit that the old man healed me. I don't feel the pain I had in my neck this morning!" I said cynically.

Despite not mentioning the pain to her before, she smiled in disbelief.

I tried not to focus on that for the moment; I was better off that way.

When the night came, I was at home doing payroll and, honestly, I had totally forgotten about Mr. Moretti and his healing spirits visiting me on that very night. I turned off my computer and went to bed.

A few minutes later, unseen forces attacked me. I tried to get up, but something pinned me down. I literally felt two invisible beings holding me down by my arms. I tried to scream but my throat hurt and couldn't utter a single word.

The attack continued. I had the sensation in my belly and chest of burning up inside and outside with fire. My mental state and my heart rate were altered. I felt as if my torso was about to blow up in pieces. I did not understand what the heck was happening to me. I knew I was fighting a spiritual battle. All I remember hearing was strange whisperings and loud squealing. I immediately felt the presence of two spirits. One of them was a female and another one was a male entity. They tried to communicate with me, but the whole thing had turned into a very violent struggle. The entities wanted to enter my flesh!

"How could this be possible?" I kept asking myself.

I went through this sort of possession during my childhood, but never as strong and compelling as that night. I was scared to death and peed in my shorts.

The challenge was so extreme. I was breathing through my anxiety; my mind was drained and weak. I couldn't think straight, and my throat would not respond to my brain in order to articulate a curse against my attackers.

I then recalled that they had tricked me. I'd accepted their proposal to take over my body, although as they tried to get inside me, my body went through a lot of physical pain as well. I heard the sound of many voices. I could only describe the loudest ones as similar to many pigs squealing in pain or fear, like pigs on their way to the slaughterhouse. I tried to scream again yet no sound came out of my mouth, and finally I felt released in an instant.

The spirits couldn't make it in, and soon enough they had to get the hell out. I did not see these spirits with my own eyes, but I had this understanding. What I remember was that they asked me if they could live within me, but my response was a loud, "No!"

Minutes later they tried to force their way into me again and complained that I couldn't break a promise.

"How did I get to know these things?" I wondered.

I am still trying to figure that out. It is not the same as seeing with one's eyes because it's not seeing clearly enough, but seeing with the spirit, which is considered a dormant knowledge within us. Something within and around me did not allow them to enter into me. I had a special seal; somehow, I did understand that there was a seal that they wouldn't be able to break. It was only natural for my spirit to know that. I learned that night that they could do things to my physical body, but they couldn't possess me totally in any way.

I heard them say to one another, "He is not belonging," as they left in fear.

The next day, I couldn't wait to get to work and tell Vicky about my extraordinary story, and as soon as I arrived, I told her what had happened to me. She was astonished at my account and a bit superstitious. I don't know if she believed me or not, but I know she feared for my spiritual well-being for what Mr. Moretti could do to me—some sort of witchery.

Mr. Moretti came by that day. When I caught sight of him, I rushed into my office, but I told Vicky to tell him that I was not available to see anyone in case he asked for me. She seemed reluctant about getting involved. I started to work and didn't want to deal with the strange old man. I had a quick glance at the monitor screen when he got into the store. I watched his every move through the security system and caught them talking very clearly, including the sound. Now he seemed a bit jumpy and somewhat upset.

After a short while, Mr. Moretti asked her about me. Vicky's response was that I was really busy doing my paperwork.

"Good job, Vicky," I said it to myself.

He kept staring into the exact camera (out of all seven) that I chose to have a better look, but he wouldn't know that, and it freaked me out.

"Well, I hope he is feeling better about that pain in the neck," he sarcastically said while gripping the cigar in the corner of his mouth.

She smiled and said nothing.

Then he continued, "Say, did your boss mention anything to you about having trouble sleeping last night?"

Vicky tried to avoid the subject at all cost, but she went on saying, "We didn't have any time to talk today yet. He's like really busy right now."

He took the cigar out of his mouth and pointed his cigar into the camera as he held it in his right hand, "Well, I got to go now. Tell him I came by to say hi, okay?!"

He paid for his gas and took off.

My mind started racing like "Uh-oh, old bastard!"

I came out of my office for a second to see his car take off. I wanted to forget the whole incident and stayed in my office for a while dealing with lots of little things to occupy my mind. I did not get back to Vicky until a couple of hours later to avoid the subject. She did not say anything. I did the same. The day went by quickly.

A few days later, I had to be in a meeting and took the whole day off. Upon my return and right before Vicky went home, she jokingly said to me, "Hey, your friend was here today asking for you."

I knew exactly what she meant, so I smiled but did not ask what friend that was. Many people ask for me all the time anyway, but I figured that it was old Mr. Moretti.

Right after she said that I was amazed to see the old man walking in with his wife through the main door.

"Honey, these are my friends," he said with a bright smile. "Carlos and Vicky and that other guy," he said in reference to Jorge, who worked the afternoon shift.

His wife was beautiful regardless of her age; she smiled and looked very charming. I shook hands with her.

Mrs. Moretti gave us a friendly hug, then she said playfully, "I hope my husband is not giving you guys a hard time. Otherwise, run him off from your store."

We laughed at her cute joke.

"Oh, honey!" he said with a smile as he held her by her waist.

The lady was a sweetheart. She had her eyes set on me. I felt uncomfortable because she saw in me something that her heart desired. I couldn't tell but she kind of freaked me out. Then, playfully she went on to explain to me that her house had a beautiful backyard.

182

Mr. Moretti jumped into the conversation and asked me if I loved nature.

"Certainly, who wouldn't?" I replied nicely.

He described the wonderful lake with a deck that highlighted their backyard. They had geese and ducklings of awesome beauty roaming around the open, natural habitat, which made the scenery desirable for anyone who would visit their home.

I was curious about their home resting by the edge of a lake. I wanted to meet them on their terms, but I also was not so open to the idea about befriending my customers. I promised myself to give it some thought.

Although Mrs. Moretti seemed mentally healthy and a very pleasant person, something was very odd about her. I felt it in my gut but wouldn't know until much later as the story unfolds.

***

As time went by and we got closer to the nice old man and his stories of his many encounters with the unknown, I had my doubts because I believe I am very intuitive. He claimed that a Native American's spirit and a young man's spirit (his wife's dead son) were always around him, yet I never felt any abnormal activity, so I wouldn't know if it was some crazy talk.

Vicky told me that she was afraid of him and didn't want to deal with him the way it was going so far. She told me that he talked to people that weren't there and asked her to greet his friends. I laughed and thought all of it was just too funny.

On other occasions when I was around Mr. Moretti, he did not talk to any of his friendly spirits nor did I feel any abnormalities around him either. I told Vicky that maybe he was playing with us or feeding off of her anxieties. One day Vicky confronted Mr. Moretti and told him playfully that when I was around, he did not talk to his friends. All he did was smile suspiciously and keep to himself. In fact, I heard him mumbling something to his unseen friends, yet he explained in detail why the spirits stayed back in his car most of the time. He said something so bogus we didn't even care.

During the next two weeks, one unexpected day Vicky asked me if she could go home early. But before she left, she told me how her day was regarding our merchants and customers; it was nothing out of the ordinary. When she left, I took over her shift.

Lately, Mr. Moretti started to visit our store almost every day. He liked to hang around and tell me about his dark stories of horror that seemed so normal to me. He usually parked his car in the same spot. We even called pump number eight his pump, but he suddenly stopped coming for a couple of weeks. Until he reappeared in the store, we never saw him. Then, one day, I turned around, and he was standing there facing me.

I greeted him cheerfully, "Hey, Mr. Moretti, what's going on, sir?"

He drew a half smile on his face. "Hey, big boss, how are you doing?" He sounded very funny but didn't smile again.

"I am doing great. What's up?"

"Oh, nothing." He was not interested in chatting; instead, he was rather forgetful. He looked at both sides over his shoulders and tried to act playfully.

"Where are your imaginary friends, Mr. Moretti?" I cynically said.

The old man got really impatient and very upset. I realized I screwed up, but it was already too late.

"I'm sorry. What did I do?" I said apologetically.

He pulled a strand of hair on his forehead towards the back of his head and sighed heavily exhaling the smell of his Cuban cigars.

"Be quiet, fool; don't let them hear you," he whispered. "These particular spirits are very sensitive. Today both of 'em are pissed off."

I played along thinking maybe he was being funny.

"Oh, I am so sorry I didn't greet George or Black Paws. Are they here now?"

Unexpectedly, the metal rack with bags of chips toppled over onto the floor.

Mr. Moretti looked at me in a strange way.

I quickly turned to look stupidly at the rack lying there with the chips spread out all over the place.

He whispered again, "Hey, be careful how you say his name. It's Black Foot, not Paws."

I got out of the cashier's booth to pick up the chips off the floor.

The old man was not even near the rack to blame him for the trick, if you could call it that.

"I'm sorry, man!" I said trying to sound apologetic with the old man.

He left the store and looked pissed.

I felt bad for a moment; I was only trying to be funny. I guess I messed it up for old Mr. Moretti. I was ashamed of myself; I hurt the old man's feelings. He was acting like a nutcase, and I didn't know how to react. The glass door closed right behind him while I was putting the chips back on the rack. I turned, and the old man was getting into his car, when for a second or two, human figures materialized right there in his car. They appeared to be sitting and staring at me. I saw them clearly: a skinny man with pigtails and another figure of what seemed to be a young guy behind the driver's seat. I jumped out of my wits when he drove off. Their eyes were on me without blinking. I kept the impression to myself and did not make any mention of this event to anyone. My left arm was shaking uncontrollably. All of that happened in bright daylight which was so unlikely, but I was getting used to the paranormal 24/7.

Later in the week, Mr. Moretti showed up again; he was his old self. He greeted me as if nothing had happened before. We started a conversation, which ended up as unusual.

As always, Vicky asked him out of the blue, "Where are your friends, Mr. Moretti?"

He smiled and replied, turning to his car, "Oh, they're inside my car. They're always with me!"

Vicky and I turned to look at his car. The car was empty. We saw nothing!

"Hey, Mr. Moretti, I would like to apologize about the other day!" I said.

He was calm about it. "It's okay," he said with a great smile.

Vicky knew, although I've said nothing to her.

I also admitted nothing.

Then, Mr. Moretti called me to the side and away from Vicky. He said quietly, "How would you like to come to my house for a celebration?"

I kept some distance from him.

"Oh, I don't know, Mr. Moretti. I have a lot of compromises lately."

I was lying because I did not want to take the risk of befriending my customer. I didn't want to be in that position. I had enough of my own psychic phenomena going on in my life already. That would probably affect me emotionally. I had nothing in common with either him or his wife, but I liked them somewhat. They were unusual. Mr. Moretti could be as old as my grandfather who passed away very young in his sixties and that was the only kind of connection I felt with him. I was not really interested to see him outside of my workplace for the obvious reasons.

He insisted that I was not going to be bored. It was like he read my thoughts. He said that his parties always included all kinds of people of different ages, and it was in honor of The Lady of Fátima.

"The Virgin of Fátima?" I asked in disbelief.

He smiled cheerfully and answered, "Yes."

I thought to myself, "Probably the devil he's talking about."

I couldn't believe he was going to celebrate a religious event in his home, especially a Catholic one, when he had claimed that he walked around with spirits and other entities and that he had conversations with the spirit world always.

"Well, let me think about it, okay?" I couldn't believe my ears that I said that.

He added, "The Feast of our Lady of Fatima is going to be on the 13th of May. That's her day, and we'll have a big celebration at home."

I turned to Vicky speechless.

"My wife is devoted to her, you know."

In my Nicaraguan culture, we also have a day to celebrate "The Immaculate Conception of The Virgin Mary." We have guests coming into our homes as well and feed them. People share treats for the little ones like fruits, candies, and toys while everyone prays and chants beautiful religious hymns to the Holy Queen of Heavens, The Mother of God.

I thought it was the same deal, so I was going to give it some thought because back in those days I was not as religious as I was when I was a kid. A whole week went by. The day prior to the engagement in his home, the old man showed up with Mrs. Moretti. She came rushing out of the car full of joy and with a big friendly smile stamped all over her face. She hugged me kindly.

"Hi there, sweetheart!"

The old lady slapped me with a peck on my cheek. She caught me off guard.

"My husband told me that he invited you to our home for the Feast of Our Lady's Celebration, is that right?"

I nodded and simply smiled at her; I knew that I never had accepted his invitation, but she continued as if I had.

"Don't you forget it's tomorrow, hon?"

And then she had a very strange request when she asked me for a small favor in consideration of the religious event.

"I would like to ask you if you can dress all in white?"

Vicky kicked my shoe under the counter and raised her eyebrows.

Mrs. Moretti insisted, "Try to wear all white if you can, in honor of our lady, OK, darling?"

I had no other option than to reply, "Certainly, ma'am, all in white. I'll do my best to comply!"

How ridiculous was that?! My mind started racing; maybe I'll make an excuse to avoid the whole thing. I knew they weren't going to miss me anyway. But life has its unexpected turns.

That night, I dreamed an unusual dream but also a very strange one indeed. I stood on a lakeshore full of white geese. The sky was bright when suddenly it turned dark and clouded with a many shades of grey. I wore a white tunic and was barefooted with beautiful green grass under my feet. As I looked around, I was surrounded by human-hybrids that looked like wolves with pointed ears. Some of them were intimidating to me while others morphed into humans. They dressed in black hooded robes and had a leather strap around their waists.

At a distance a very bright star shone over the waters at the edge of the lake. It illuminated me and shined down upon the faces of the crowd of humans, animals, or both! When what looked like a miraculous or strange event started to take place, the impossible happened. Animals and humans interbred with wolves, and their eyes reflected in the dark with golden tones. They all turned in my direction. I was mesmerized with the horrific spectacle.

All of us felt the need to wade inside the crystalline lake waters. I felt that my white robe was getting soaked by the water which had turned muddy. The abomination of creatures was already ahead of me. I was the last one to go into the lake, and then I heard howling. The geese suddenly dropped dead from the sky into the riverbank. Their heads were cut off, and their bodies were covered in blood. Some of the blood was dripping from above and all over the beautiful green grass.

I tried to go further like everyone else to get near the bright star. I was curious and wanted to see what that light was all about. As I stood in the shallow waters, I began to sink into mud, and when I tried to take another step, my feet got caught in the weeds at the bottom of the lake, perhaps in algae. My clothes were all muddy, and I couldn't move. I cried out for help, but no one seemed to care. I kept sinking in. I felt hopeless and about to drown.

"What a horrible death!" I thought to myself.

I woke up sweating and breathing heavily. I stayed in my bed for a while thinking what all of that meant. I put everything in the back of my mind.

Next day, May 13th, the day of the celebration at the Morettis' home, I wasn't excited at all. I was really anxious with so many negative things happening all at the same time in my head. I also had a lot of work to do and wasn't going to put any thoughts about my dream into this event. Not only that, I kept it to myself; I did not want to sound like a loony in despair. So, I worked harder to forget it. I could take my mind off the deranged subject, but that day was not an easy day for me. I had to tackle a lot of delayed paperwork. Not only that but my boss called me for an unexpected lunch meeting. I took off around eleven that morning. The meeting was a waste of time including some of the corporation's marketing ideas. It was just another boring day on the job.

My boss was talking, and my mind was somewhere in la-la-land, so far away in my thoughts. I couldn't get the Morettis' event off my mind. I was intrigued by my dream as well. It was so real, but I could not interpret its meaning or a message. What if my life was in jeopardy? Most of the time my dreams were not just simple; they always talked to me, and I knew that. There were too many symbols in them. I used to write about my dreams in a book, but they were countless, and I got tired of doing that.

When the meeting was over, I didn't feel like stopping by my store, so I went straight home. I called my employees and talked to Vicky for a little while about the meeting and told her that I was gone for the day.

I was about to hang up the phone when she quickly said, "Mr. Moretti came down and asked for you. His wife seemed very interested that you not miss their Santeria party."

"Celebration," I corrected her. Then I said to her "Since it is about the virgin, didn't they ask you to go? They know you are a religious person."

"Not really. They do not consider me their friend, you know."

"Nonsense, I wonder why they did not invite you?"

"Well, actually, I am glad I was not invited. I was not going to go anyway."

"Why is that?"

"I would be afraid to go. Hope you get the hint!"

"Are you crazy? I'm more positive now about going because if the devil really does exist, I will meet him tonight."

Vicky fussed a little and went on and on about the devil's tricks on people like me, "Oh, my God, you're crazy, you know. I hope you're kidding."

"Sorry, I just made up my mind, so if you see me all messed up in my head tomorrow, you'll know what happened to me, okay?"

I was messing with Vicky; I liked to see her freaking out.

Back in my apartment that night, I went straight to bed and relaxed for a while trying to put all my problems behind me. I was trying to deny my wanting to go to the Moretti's Santeria event. I did not know what to expect. Even my dreams did not seem positive.

Still, I was interested in going. Mr. Moretti's last conversation with me was about claiming the virgin always performed a miracle in his home, and that many people got to see her in all her splendor. With that being said, I was positive about two things: if it wasn't alien-related, then it had to be the devil itself, and if the devil, then there was truly a God. I was trying to convince myself that it was an alien-related case because I am an experiencer of these phenomena. The bright star setting on the lake in my dreams only meant a sign for me. However, I did not know what to make of it. I was more confused. Should I trust that old man? I doubted a lot of things in my head already.

The invitation was for 7 PM until midnight. I looked through my clothes to see if I could find any white shirts or white pants. I had none, so I dressed in black; I had lots of black.

I drove my way to the Morettis. I arrived in no time. I saw a bunch of cars parked around a pretty nice house probably built in the 1950s or '60s. The whole neighborhood was very well taken care of with lots of plants and nicely manicured green grass. The backyard was surrounded by a wooden picket fence, and there was a doorbell on the gate. I parked and waited inside my SUV to follow the drill, and it was exactly as I thought. A few minutes later, I got out of my vehicle. I had not gotten near the gate when Mr. Moretti came out to meet me, shaking my hand and leading me through the main entrance. He was very cheerful and made me feel welcome.

"Thank you, sir," I said smiling.

"You are a privileged person and our special guest tonight. You should enter like royalty."

I thought that he was making fun of me when I noticed all the people there looked very important. I was a nobody and technically, not even their friend, but he was dead serious. I really did not care; I was going to play his way to see what to expect at his home that night.

We sat in his living room, and he filled me in on what to expect in the celebration. I was impressed about his claims. Mr. Moretti was at ease, calmly opening up to me, and told me about spirits, souls, spiritual trances, and such. I thought I was hearing myself talking. For a moment I realized how crazy everything he had said to me sounded, yet I knew in my heart he wasn't lying one bit. I tried to keep calm, hold my laughter, get a hold of myself, and not show any negative emotions. Nevertheless, I disrespected that man with my attitude of disbelief. No matter how promising it all sounded, it's not the same. I've been going through this all my life, and now that I am around people who believed in this stuff, I couldn't envision myself being a part of it. But I did listen to the old man very carefully for the most part.

The crowd was formed of all types of people dressed in all white and already gathering in his patio, enjoying great music and helping themselves to all kinds of foods, snacks and alcoholic drinks. The Morettis had a nice, huge patio with a big oak tree overlooking the lake.

"Damn, he had a lake in his backyard, and there was a dock with ducklings and geese all over the place!" I thought in my head. It was exactly as I had dreamt it.

People were arranged in different groups. I felt like a dead fly floating on top of a glass of milk.

He looked at my black clothes and said, "It's okay to wear black, too." Then he gave me a naughty look jokingly.

I felt a bit embarrassed but, hey, it was too late to do anything about that.

"Let me find you a nice spot and introduce you to some very nice people."

We walked around, and at the very first table, I got introduced to a couple of guys that claimed they were doctors from a local known hospital. After that, a few lawyers got together with us; we were the singles. According to their conversation, I did not doubt their profession. They were very articulate and intelligent people with a vast knowledge of things that did convince me they were whom they claimed to be. As for that night, they talked about the prior year's celebration and many marvelous things that happened. I knew that night was not going to be an exception. I was ready to live through it with at least a hundred witnesses. I couldn't wait!

Thirty minutes into the night the place was fully packed. At around 8 PM everyone that needed to be there was already within the crowd. It got dark very soon, but not quite as one would expect; there was a little bit of brightness still. A band played Latin Salsa, and some woman asked me to dance. I declined very nicely.

"I stop dancing a long time ago," I said with a smirk, and in my head, I thought, "No one is going to make me dance."

She smiled and seemed puzzled as if she had read my mind. She then went to an older gentleman who went along with her. He had the moves. A bunch of octogenarian couples, very old looking people, appeared out of nowhere. Their skin was pale, very pale like corpses. It was the strangest thing I'd ever seen in my very conscious state. They were dancing so strangely to a new song that also blended in unsuspiciously; it was quite the show. They moved weirdly, like ancient tribal dancers performing rituals. I was amazed for their age. I also thought that it was odd to have that kind of pagan music for a Christian celebration, unless of course that event had nothing Catholic about it.

"Bottom's up hard liquor galore was being served as the main entry and at a religious celebration?" I kept asking myself with a funny, stupid smile on my face.

The servers went around with very large trays of whiskey, beer, wine, and you name it, just the way mundane people like it. I liked it, and I was mundane, but it felt totally wrong having the sacred image of Our Lady of Fatima standing in the middle of that gathering. The whole picture was taking form: a true shade of gray. Like I've said before, I wasn't as religious anymore, yet, it felt wrong in my heart.

The waiters and waitresses wore formal uniforms. The buffet table had big trays of delicious, hot food. I spotted also a humongous barrel full of ice with all types of beer. We got thirsty at my table, so each one of us got up and walked to the barrel to grab some more cold ones. I got my beer of choice, a few Coronas, and drank them as fast as they came.

Most guests were regulars to the event, and they talked about their previous paranormal accounts at the Morettis. From what I gathered in their conversations, the past year's events were full of marvelous experiences. Some others kept to themselves and did not comment about anything, especially with me. I guess they saw me as an outsider. They seemed to be guarding some sort of a secret. I was positive I was going to have an encounter of some sort, but I never expected what was coming next. All I had was my nightmare as a reference.

Mrs. Moretti grabbed a microphone. Her hair was still dripping wet as she looked like she just stepped out of a shower. She greeted and thanked the crowd for making it to the event. Then she pointed to the sacred image of the Virgin of Fatima surrounded by a bunch of fresh flowers forming a niche around it. I missed it before because it was placed in a blind spot. Mr. Moretti got closer to her, and they both continued with the greetings. A chubby woman next to them was providing all sorts of information and dates as they needed to explain whatever they had to share with the crowd. I'll admit that whatever they had to say the crowd would be very interested, and I was very impressed with their submissive attitude.

In a funny way, Mrs. Moretti was straight forward saying that she had just come out of the shower, was receiving messages from the virgin herself in her bedroom, and that is why she took a little longer to come and greet all of us but couldn't wait any longer.

I was like, "She's nuts! Damn!" in a cute sort of way.

That lady was not the same coherent person I met at my store a few days before. She seemed to be in another realm. That night Mrs. Moretti looked paranoid while her husband clapped and cheered. What a show!

People all around were truly into their weird, crazy talk like sheep until the Morettis finally finished. Everyone clapped and agreed with Mrs. Moretti's claims. I couldn't believe my eyes and ears about this whole thing, but, hey, I also knew, metaphorically speaking, that I had a piece of the same pie with my very own experiences. I could not totally dismiss the fact of their unusual claims. Instead, these people were giving me a chance to belong and to have some sort of a unique experience in their company surrounded by many witnesses. Perhaps I was in denial about who I was. I had to belong there and was not seeing myself being a part of the "crazies," as the world would judge them. The world would crucify me as a loony, but here I was with the people who belonged to my club, and I felt totally the opposite.

All of my life, I have been hiding my stories or fixing them up in a way so that people could relate to them without giving me "the look." Now, I was in the same place where others had judged me so hard during my life, and I was doing what I learned from them: to judge others harshly. Therefore, I tried not to be judgmental about them in any way. I switched to using my paranormal mode, so I could feel at ease and forget completely about my typical logic. My reasoning was to keep my feet on the ground for this time only.

The Morettis made it clear with their guests about having a lot of fun by drinking and dancing to the celebration.

"The virgin would appreciate it!" Mr. Moretti said, as if the Holy Mother of God was one of his drinking buddies.

Mrs. Moretti whispered into the mic holding the thing very close to her face, "I'm gonna let you in on a little secret, people."

The crowd stayed still and listened quietly.

I was astonished with the circus. The more she talked, the more everything seemed so farfetched.

"What role was I playing?" I kept asking myself. "Was I the only one seeing what I saw? Or was it my contaminated mind?"

I was fighting one of the biggest battles in my life: manipulation, mass hypnosis, or plain crazy people enjoying a madness day without the need to use any psychedelic drugs.

"The Lady of Fatima is already here!" said Mrs. Moretti as she jumped on one foot holding herself on the chubby woman's shoulder, the one called Irma.

The woman helped Mrs. Moretti fix one of her shoes that came loose from her foot with a price tag still attached to the bottom of the sole.

"Oh, my goodness!" everyone croaked.

"She asked me to tell you," Irma said with a straight face, "that she is a bit tired from traveling all the way from Portugal and that she would soon join us after she has rested for a short while."

Everyone clapped.

I was dumbfounded. I couldn't believe what I was hearing: a spirit resting.

"That'll be the day!"

What was worse was the crowd believing her comments at face value. I got myself a couple of beers but this time with a shot of Tequila, raw sea salt, and a wedge of lemon so as to be on the same page with the crowd. Maybe that is what I needed to do in order to understand a lot better what was going on that night.

Mr. Moretti showed up with a glass of whisky in his hand.

"This is my favorite time of the event. Here, take this," he said with a smirk on his face and handed me the drink.

I didn't hesitate and gulped the booze quickly.

He smiled and said, "Hey, enjoy your drinks as much as you wish; otherwise, I may run out sooner than expected." He slapped me on the back and left.

At this point, the other guys at my table were already in some sort of a trance. How weird! When I turned, everyone else was also under the same spell. I was not, so I thought.

Irma grabbed the mic, and everyone turned to her.

"I have a message from the virgin herself."

Everyone was so quiet you could hear a pin drop.

I decided to walk down to the dock near the lake next to the single people. We were in the middle of a lame conversation when everyone around stopped talking all of a sudden, all of them at once. I had a cold beer in my hand and gulped it faster.

Then, the unexpected happened.

Irma points out in my direction and said, "You."

Every eye was on me. She kept pointing her finger at me. I never thought she really referred to me exactly, so I looked away.

A female's voice from within the crowd near me said, "Mister, it's you she's calling."

I looked away to avoid eye contact. I was still in disbelief.

A guy next to me turned towards me and clearly said, "It's you she is pointing to, man!"

I was stone cold when I saw her calling me using the mic and asking the Morettis for my name. I did not know what the hell she wanted from me. I had too many beers already; I wasn't prepared for anything let alone a conversation in public having the whole crowd as witnesses. Perhaps that was only a joke from that crazy old-timer, Mr. Moretti, and he put me on the spot using Irma!

So, I walked back up to Irma, and she put the mic away.

People went back to whatever they were doing before.

Good God, I wasn't in the spotlight any longer. I felt better.

"The Virgin wants to have a word with you."

"What?!" I replied swallowing a big gulp, and then I thought to myself, "The devil wants me. He wants to talk to me!"

I then thought that was just plain ridiculous, so I challenged the devil by following after the annoying woman who seemed disoriented. Walking through the crowd, I got to see a better picture of the whole thing. No one looked like ordinary people; they were more like in a dark cult of some sort. But, hey, I was there and I was going to go through with it. I couldn't just back away from it. That wasn't me! No sir, I was not stepping back like a coward.

So, I followed Irma into the living room. She told me to sit in a chair, and I did. The damn crystal chandeliers started to shake and make that noise crystals do when they get moved around and touch each other. When I looked up nothing moved any longer. I tried to look for a fish line but nothing was attached to the lamp. Next, the lights sparkled on and off for seconds at a time, and I thought that probably the A/C coming from the roof grills did all of that but that was impossible. The grill was in another part of the living room. At that very moment, hot air blew from the floor onto my feet. I looked under me, and there were no signs of any heater grill or any ventilation at all. I looked everywhere and felt both cold and hot air both at the same time. I figured out that I had experienced the weirdest thing ever. Very odd indeed.

Irma got closer and said, "Concentrate, mister, concentrate."

I can't remember a time when I had to concentrate to experience any paranormal activity around me ever. Irma was right next to me, grabbed me by my shoulder, and then all hell broke loose. I heard a whirlwind whistle around me. I knew for a fact that nothing could do such a thing. I doubted any paranormal activity because my body usually goes through a cold sweat mode. I had none of that at that time. I smelled a trick, so I kept still when suddenly a shadowy silhouette appeared and stood by the window across from me. It appeared to move in my direction.

Irma moved away and left me alone.

I looked around and didn't see a living soul other than me in the living room. Even if I couldn't see, I could feel a thing was roaming around the whole room, an unseen force getting stronger by the minute. I did feel its presence. That's when a solid image appeared. A dark winged entity similar to a black bag, a rag, or a bat, yet huge in size, flew right up to the wall across from me. That truly threw me off because it was very solid to me. It had intelligence and happened in plain sight.

My heart was racing, I tried to get the hell out; I had had enough for one day. I was stuck in the chair, and my emotions inside were building up, yet I couldn't get up or scream or do anything. I saw everyone through the glass sliding doors that faced the patio. People were having a good time while I was trapped and frightened. The music played loud, but the noise in my head seemed to have been reduced to a minimum, as if I were an object. That effect was not observing the laws of physics because one of the glass doors was still open.

"How was that even possible?" I thought to myself.

The music band still played their instruments and sang. I knew something was wrong with that picture. What I did was what I always do in situations where I can't control my surroundings and my body won't obey my mind. I tried not to think about it, tried to get up, and get out. That was when I started to experience all sorts of visual lights, bogus sounds, and what I always expect in the end: the cold sweats and the shivering.

The kitchen window with a double glass which slides up and down shook like a loose pressure cooker valve, building up where the glass took the shape of a balloon, as if it would burst at any time. It was clear that there was no trick, and I knew it. I thought of all the possibilities as well. Maybe someone had dropped a drug on my drink, but I knew for a fact that I picked up my beers randomly. No one ever offered me one, but then I recalled Mr. Moretti giving me a glass with whiskey earlier.

"Damn, the old dude slipped a drug in my drink!" I thought.

I knew I was trying to pin my experiences on something or someone. I knew I had no drugs in that drink. Suddenly, I heard a noise right behind me, a sound which pierced right through my ears and made me cringe like a metallic engine of sorts and then followed by a human, "Hush." I jumped out of my wits, dropping my beer on the carpet and grabbing my head.

"Phew!"

I freed myself from that damn chair and walked out towards the crowd.

Irma came rushing out of nowhere and yelled, "Where are you going, mister?"

I already was pretty upset; I didn't want that weirdo on my back. I would never accept in my right mind to have any exchange with evil or something that did not look officially extraterrestrial or spiritual at a divine goodness level—that included communication with a ghost or whatever that could trick me into letting it attach itself to my physical body for the rest of my life. It was not strong enough, and I couldn't risk carrying a curse by getting infested with this sort of evil.

I have no idea why I went back to my table, but the truth was that in my head, I knew I wanted to run the hell out of that mad house, but I didn't. I wanted to experience it with the crowd. I had my bad moments before on my own, and that was very scary, but now I had the chance to share my fears with others who seemed not afraid, not one bit. I thought that I should be a little more patient and see the conclusion of this evil worship, or whatever it was.

Mr. Moretti's Cult

Irma was obviously upset, and I saw her talking to some elderly ladies. They had an evil smile on their pale faces. They whispered something back to her and turned to stare at me. Irma walked back inside the house scratching her head and disappeared from my sight.

Everyone around my table was gone—"poof"—as if it were a magic trick.

"Jesus! When did it happen?" I wondered.

I took a look around, and they were already mixed within the crowd.

There was this old man, a gringo, with a full white beard and a straw hat, and he said to me, "You lucky son-of-a-gun. You got to meet her, huh?"

I'd usually be smiling when things like this happened, but for some reason, I was a little confused by the fact that the guy had a red Hawaiian shirt on and a pair of shorts; he didn't seem to fit into the scenery of events. One thing that bothered me was that I couldn't remember ever seeing that man during the evening. How strange that was!

"Who?" I replied with a strange face.

I was playing the fool to get to the bottom of the whole mystery, but the old-timer turned and looked at the lake with a dumb ass smile. Soon enough, he vanished into thin air— "poof"—gone! I was impressed; my mind was trying to assimilate the phenomena, perhaps a trick of the mind. Or my own perception, who knows?!

At the dock I got to see the geese, the swan, and the ducklings swimming alone with their little chicks on the lake in harmony.

One thing led to another when a commotion back in the house took place. Mrs. Moretti stood facing the crowd. She took the microphone again and started to yell at the top of her lungs with excitement. Crazy bitch, she scared the living daylights out of me.

"Split up y'all! There she is!"

201

The crowd split apart up the middle into two groups. It felt as if we were being forced to move by something greater than our own will.

The old woman quickly pointed towards the far end of the lake. She had quite the smile, showing her perfect white teeth.

"I present to you the Lady of Fatima."

Her hands were shaking, and my head started rushing with many thoughts.

To this day, I still can't believe how the crowd parted in the middle the same way Moses parted the Red Sea with the power of God on his side, surreal and magically. It was amazing. I felt as if an invisible force levitated us. We appeared to be placed to the sides leaving an empty space in between all the way to the house.

Lights flashed inside the water. They were self-contained, violent bubbles that seemed to boil up from the bottom of the lake. Something was trying to materialize but didn't as if a huge whale were about to jump out of the water.

My breathing got heavier. My heart pumped so hard that I felt it in my mouth. My alcohol level was gone.

"Come out, you coward," I kept repeating that in my head.

There was excitement on everyone's face. They were continuously clapping. The strangest thing ever was to see the crowd in the same spirit, which I wasn't sharing, because I was in total control. I had a conscience and was analyzing the whole event, yet I moved in slow motion for some reason.

All the homes around the lake, at least twenty-five of them, that I had seen upon my arrival were in the dark. No one seemed to be around the lake but the Morettis' guests.

I wasn't a believer at all about Mary's appearances, but I was no fool. I knew for a fact that it was not a Mary miracle. Why do I say this? Because I was in fear and nothing matched any godly inspiration I had ever learned during my childhood through my Catholic faith. I knew that the EVIL ONE himself with tail and horns was going to make his flamboyant entrance for his privileged children and helped by his followers, his countless fallen angels.

Then nothing!

What a fiasco: the devil remained in the shadows and wouldn't come out of the waters.

It was already dark all around. Some lights were seen in the shallow waters, more like something illuminating that side of the lake. The wind blew in circles on the treetops; perhaps a mini storm is a better definition. Some of the branches bent down as if the trees were made of rubber. You couldn't be certain of what really went on anymore. Some noise that came with the storm sounded like a dying engine.

Did they put on a show for me? I don't think so.

Mrs. Moretti passed out right in front of the crowd. Some elderly women assisted her, grabbed her by the arms, and helped her to sit in a padded chair.

At that point, Irma started to scream like a wild-caged animal.

I don't recall if I wanted to clap with laugher, yet in my mind what just happened with Mrs. Moretti felt like she deserved it. I wanted to praise her dramatic act, like one that belonged to a badly written novel, but for the adrenaline rush, I would certainly clap and scream "Brava" after all. I felt as if I were seeing the end of "Madame Butterfly" in the opera house somewhere in New York. Instead, I knew I was petrified, not out of fear, but because who could do these things in real life? Who had the power to use human emotions, interfere with reality, and also use the wind, the waters, and hypnotize people like I saw that night? Who do I know can put on the greatest show on earth and confuse the minds of those who walk around and know nothing of lies and deceptions? Only The Evil One, Satan the Deceiver.

I thought to myself, "What if these people were putting on a show for me and played me for a fool? Damn, if that were so, then they were better than all those tricks at Universal Studios and cost me nothing."

I looked around for the special effects boxes or any signs of them but nothing—no cables, no guys around looking or acting weird. I detected no trickery. I am a guy who pays attention to details, but I found nothing that would make me consider what I witnessed at the Morettis was illegitimate or fake, unless I was a total fool.

After the greatest live show I had ever seen in my life, everyone there gathered around exhausted and confused. My hands shook like leaves.

I kept repeating in my head, "What the heck happened, really?!"

Mrs. Moretti came back around from her sensationally dramatic scene. She discussed something in a very low voice with the women around her. She started to cry inconsolably and grabbed the microphone one last time. Mr. Moretti joined her and repeated her words in agony.

"People, we would like to apologize for what you just witnessed, but there was a very serious situation that happened just now."

Everyone was silent and paid careful attention to the Morettis.

Mr. Moretti took the mic from her because she couldn't stop crying and said the craziest thing I have ever heard during my life in this world.

"The virgin was kidnapped," he said while he sniffed and pulled a white handkerchief out of his pockets, "by some bad, bad, evil spirits."

Now he was crying like a little boy.

He went on, "She won't be able to escape from them tonight."

To my amazement everyone was crying and banging on the tables in distress.

"For God's sake!"

It was a madhouse. What a drama! There was absolutely no logic behind any of it. The whole thing was impossible to believe with my human logic. I couldn't understand anything at all. I had had more than enough for that night.

I got up from the chair very slowly. I walked past people hoping no one would notice me and left quietly into the night.

I was about to enter my SUV when the old man in the Hawaiian shirt reappeared nearby the line of parked cars.

"Lucky son-of-a-gun, I can see you escaped unharmed!"

I foolishly smiled and said nothing, but I did give him the thumbs up and quickly jumped into my car. I had forgotten he had vanished previously right before my eyes.

Thank God that any other vehicle had not blocked my car. Before I left, I looked back at the Morettis one last time. I could finally breathe. The music kept playing ancient rhythms with bongos. I turned my car on and without giving it another thought, I split silently into the night.

I kept saying to myself, "Thank you, God. I'm alive and well, thank you."

***

My life that night was at risk, and I don't know why I had that feeling. Something really evil was present in that place, and I knew I was not prepared to be someone's sacrifice. I felt like I'd exposed my life in that place! So, I kind of pushed the whole thing to the back of my mind and forgot about it like many other experiences I would prefer to keep out of reach.

***

Mr. Moretti disappeared after that for a while, and then one day, out of the blue, he showed up at the store all dazed and confused. He didn't talk much. He paid in advance $100 dollars to fill up his tank and left without filling up with any gas at the pump! His wife came in hours later; she was a mess. She was trembling, almost on the verge of crying, and desperately asking if we had seen her husband.

Vicky comforted her. We gave her a bottle of water, explained to her what had happened to Mr. Moretti, and of course, returned his money to her!

Mrs. Moretti went on to say that he had not been back to the store because all of a sudden he had lost his memory from one day to the next and disappeared all day. She had to go to all the places he frequented to find him and bring him home. He was also pulling hundreds of dollars from the bank and returning empty-handed.

After that day (two to three months after the event), we never saw the Morettis again, and I certainly wasn't going to his home to find out why after my negative experience. He vanished from our minds until I moved to Los Angeles.

***

Years later, I realized that the Morettis were setting me up to become possessed by the demon presence I felt while being held down in the chair in the living room. It was all part of joining Mr. Moretti's cult of possessed humans, some of whom looked like the walking dead to me. By possessing me, I would then become a puppet and be able to corrupt others to the dark side. The whole affair might have been retribution by the two "ghosts," whom I belittled earlier in the store, prompting them to throw down my chip display in anger. When I resisted the "two ghosts" from possessing me that one time at night, they decided to punish me further by setting me up with a really nasty demon possession. Luckily, I kept my wits about me and was defiant enough to get away from the cult party because I always believed that I was protected by some kind of a seal and a positive energy signature. Plus, my nightmare about getting stuck in the mud of the lake while the geese fell to Earth all bloody was a clairvoyant vision warning me about the event, similar to the clairvoyant vision I had warning me about 9/11 in "The Death of the Innocents."

14.

Mrs. Farnsworth's Rhapsody

"We are here," she said, "to help those who want to be helped."

"Don't worry. It's not going to hurt you!"

My eyes peeled right after I heard this echoing voice in my head.

"What?"

My room was completely lit up like sunlight coming through the solid walls. Then a black liquid dropped from the ventilation screen on top of the ceiling. I was static and couldn't move a finger.

"Jesus, what is that?"

That was exactly a liquid that morphed into a mechanical spider, one with long, sharp legs. I could hear the "tick, tick" speeding up towards me. My whole body was completely stiff as if I were dead. The horrible robotic insect was skillful and quickly got to me. It was a cold night, and I had my heavy blankets covering me totally but my head. The scary-looking critter walked over my blankets, and I felt the little tips of its legs running until it got to the left side of my throat.

I was short of breath and wanted to scream so my wife could wake up and help me get that horrible thing away from me or at least scare it by screaming, but the arachnid sat on an angle and stung me. I felt the sharp short needle cut through my skin very skillfully, but it did hurt like a real sting. I felt liquid being deposited and rushing through my veins. I blacked out facing my wife, who never moved a finger.

A black void calmed me down and made time run faster than a g-force. Soon, I was rushing through a tunnel full of lights and had the feeling of maximum speed, which awakened me intermittently as I passed out over and over until I arrived at my final destination.

Then the questioning began. "What am I doing here? Where is this place that looks like a futuristic hospital?"

I wasn't certain because my vision was somewhat blurry still. I expected to see all kinds of nursing personnel, doctors, and what not, if I really were in a hospital. To my amusement, strange little people seemed to be waiting with me and weren't surprised at all. It was like they were expecting all us travelers.

I would like to mention that, first of all, I was in shock, and I kept saying to myself, ***"This is a nightmare. It's not possible! Oh, God, not again!"***

I turned my face away just like when I go to the dentist. The place was full of little creatures with overgrown heads. I knew who they were already from my hidden memories and that they were the famous aliens every believer has heard or read about. My mind was alert and as usual paying attention to every detail, observing what they did to us, or what is it that they wanted from us. My mind just wanted to have a clear picture of their intentions, but my sight was still disturbed. I felt nauseated for a few minutes, and that distorted me enough to quit trying to figure anything out.

As my vision sharpened up a bit, their features became more obvious. I was not hallucinating; it was not a dream; I wasn't imagining all this again. One of the faces shocked me as not what I expected to see; in an instant, it was right there in front of me.

"A humanoid! Oh, God, another unforgettable experience!" I thought as I looked around.

Humans were in the minority.

I laughed in my head and thought, "No human is ever going to believe this. No one! No sir, they will call me a nut case, but hey, I don't care."

This experience, despite all the trauma I always go through, gave me the truth behind the mystery about extraterrestrial life. All humans dream to know if there's life besides ours. Indeed, there is, right in front of my face! Look at the zoo here! I know I had a funny smile on my face, and the humanoids could care less what went on in my head at that moment. They were busy looking for something in their computer systems. I suppose I could only guess what I thought I was seeing up to that point. My Catholic faith was definitely challenged because for some reason humans

210

always believe that they are the center of the universe. If there were any others in the universe, how come they did not try to communicate with us beforehand?

My logic kept questioning my reason. Fear was multiplying my trauma by the hundreds. I guess the effect of the drug was already wearing out. I took my time looking around at the elegant but strong, steel confinement. The place had symbols on the walls that lit up and seemed to be made of an indescribable precious metal. My impression of the symbols was that they were numbers. But I was only guessing. I knew I was not exactly what they thought of me —those darned, advanced, little, ugly people! Then, the marks or symbols reminded me of hieroglyphs.

I believe that they could read my mind literally, but they wouldn't care what I had to say or think.

Next, a comforting and reassuring voice said to me, *"You're not in danger; everything is going to be all right."*

They were soothing words that comforted and relaxed me from my shivering and frightening experience. My hidden memories came to light in my head, and I don't recall a single time when I wasn't scared to death. The truth is that our minds are willing to learn, listen, and act with reasoning, but our bodies aren't. That is so ridiculous and just the way it's always been.

Slowly, I moved my eyes to observe their work. I avoided their faces; I did not want to look at their faces, no. It freaked me out to know that behind those faces there was a thinking brain, and thoughts. I was indeed really scared to death despite being there countless times since my very first memories.

My eyes focused when my brain automatically sent an order to pay attention to the texture of their suits. I didn't think about anything else. In an experience, I always look for that kind of thing. It's the only thing that doesn't make me frightened about the situation at a certain moment in time. My eyes now zoomed into the texture, which was of a metallic material like gold foils, but it didn't stretch as a smart suit to fit anyone who wears it. It did wrap around and cover their ridiculous-looking bodies. They wore jumpsuits, not like astronaut's suits, but more similar to air force pilot's suits without any visible seams. They could have been uniforms because they had different patterns and colors. I noticed that they changed like chameleons to make a tight fit.

The circumference of what I thought was a flying craft was probably no more than 12 yards in diameter. But then again, I could have been wrong because when I was taken into another room, my impression totally changed to a humongous size. There was no way I could tell how much bigger this new room was anyway. It was a giant-sized room with very high spaces in between. I was dumbfounded; I gave up making any assumptions of what I thought I saw anymore.

My mind insisted on staring at their gliding suits, now with golden tones. I had this crazy feeling, as if I were lying down on some sort of flat bed with a soft metal but without a cushion. I had the impression that I sank in sometimes, and other times, I felt that I was in between a cushion or in midair regardless of seeing no cushion at all. My mind realized that I was not in a flatbed; it was a seat, more like a human sofa or a recliner chair.

"How did I get there without remembering the trajectory?" I thought.

I got there by … no … the truth was that I did not see it; I can't remember for sure. One more thing I don't recall was if what I thought to be a craft ever moved at all. I never even remembered if I heard any type of noise either. Next, a whooping feeling very calmly made a sound like something that sticks to a glass … yes, yes … just like a suction cup but more fragile, a delicate movement that emitted that sort of sound.

Mrs. Farnsworth's Rhapsody

Now I knew I was drugged up because they told me to stand to see if I could do it on my own, but I couldn't. I was scared to fall on my face. I was light-headed; I was very dazed and unstable. So, two very tall, skinny, white pale beings came towards me, and I was supported by my armpits to walk to another room. I was traumatized by the yucky feeling of their leathery, long fingers grabbing me under my arms. A horrid feeling revolved in my mind. I saw a whole bunch of the same beings. They wore different colored suits; these suits would not change like the others, in color that is … not like the first beings I encountered, those suits glittered.

This is where the perspective of the craft size changed in dimensions. Once in there, I felt like I was inside a large domed building of incredible dimensions with some mighty walls, as I explained previously. I wanted to make sure I mentioned this again, because for some reason, that is important for me to discuss. The architectural designs made no sense to me. I was surrounded by very large courts and some lesser courts inside them, just like in the Russian *matryoshka dolls*.

These new beings I encountered as I was being carried like a dummy never cared to even look in my direction. Despite that, I was both happy and frightened, like a morbid masochist. I wanted to go with them and I didn't want to go with them. I had great curiosity for knowing more and learning more.

Now I got better, and I could walk on my own. I walked side by side with the beings, one on each side of me. Sometimes they yanked me, and it hurt because I started gazing and slowing down. These monkeys with a suit had no patience! I felt like I wasn't even walking. I could feel my feet clinging sometimes, and an electrifying feeling ran all over my whole body. I had the impression that I was being abused when they lifted me off the floors without warning. I thought about speaking my mind and using a few profane words to complain to their superior.

A voice kept saying, "Easy, everything is going to be all right."

But this is one of those times I knew I should observe more and keep my opinions to myself, and I did.

Soon enough, I knew it was going to happen, and I hated it so much. I felt stupid. I felt like a dumb insect because I blinked and "*bang*," I found myself under observation: what humans call a complete physical performed by a human doctor. Instead of the human interaction, I felt more like a lesser being. I started to experience shortness of breath and shivering all over again.

Now my brain started with the questioning again. Along with it came the cold sweat and the euphoric feeling all over.

"Who is this man? What does he want with me? Is he a real human?"

Jesus! I was in chaos, and then the human man (doctor) without any expression gave me a shot. I never felt the needle but knew it was a sharp object. I started to smile again and gained some confidence. I wasn't scared anymore.

Suddenly, a warm, little hand, like a child's tiny hand, landed delicately on my right shoulder, and I felt safe, very safe. I tried to see whose hand was on my shoulder.

A telepathic message indicated to me, "I am here now, you are safe, and it will all be over soon!"

And I did calm down indeed!

I had a feeling deep inside that I knew this being. It was complicated; I felt a maternal sentiment coming from what seemed to be a female being by her attitude, someone I kind of knew but wasn't so human. Once she gained my trust, I suppose, she finally faced me.

In my mind I heard her call my name, and I immediately relaxed. I became at ease and I knew I had to trust the voice. To my astonishment, she appeared in front of me as if floating in a lotus position, but in my condition, it could have been an illusion. She appeared to be spinning alien symbols around in a circle, but that may have been my telepathic perception along with seeing her floating in front of me. Later on, I saw those same symbols lit up like lights on the walls of the ship.

I was upset, confused, but calm. I had the need to bitch and complain, but her first words to me were that she knew how I felt and that I was safe and everything was going to be all right. My palpitations, my anxieties, and my fears vanished as soon as I heard her speak. She spoke clearly in English, perfect English. Although I felt I spoke the same language, I realized that there was no language, but an understanding. Regardless, her voice was of a human female, and I felt that way about her. She talked or communicated, and I was acting like a babe who felt no malice. I was all trusting and also felt safe but still curious, very curious. Thousands of questions came into my head, and without saying a word, each one had an answer that came directly from her mind.

She was a tiny creature, very thin and pale, so pale that she was whiter than an albino human. Her eyes were colored, and I would be lying if I mentioned the true color, but I knew they were between hazel and blue as we know them in our world. Her mouth had lips, but it was a tiny mouth, like a doll. Her nose was tiny but looked very human. Her ears were also tiny compared to the size of her pear-shaped head. No hair anywhere. Her hands were elongated and looked human, except she seemed to be missing a finger. This doesn't mean I had not seen others that had six fingers in their hands; that was in other abductions. The being seemed to have teeth and a tongue, but also, I couldn't be sure of that because in my mind those things were normal in someone that looked like her.

I also remembered that she was a delicate being that made very soft and tender movements. She was more like the prima donna of the ballet when dancing during the mesmerizing scene of **Tchaikovsky's** most dramatic Swan Lake finale.

She had on a jumpsuit uniform of some sort. At first, she looked naked, but then I could see her uniform was as soft and tender as a baby's skin yet similar looking to metallic foils, weird to describe. She had some strange looking boots with some ancient designs resembling those of the Incas. She also had what looked like a brooch on her uniform. I thought that it was a brooch; it was not. It was something electronic that changed colors from bluish to reddish to fuchsia—a communicator of sorts or a protector. I could not figure it out. She also had some decorations on her wrists like bracelets but they also had a function. Nothing she wore was for luxury and had a useful usage for her mission.

A sordid, ultrasonic sound, more like a ringing sound, kept me under some sort of control. I call it a spell. I was analyzing everything that happened to me up to that moment, so I could easily remember. I know it happens every time when I see the *other beings that scare me*.

The female being stood up and came closer, yet she still seemed to be floating in front of me. The ringing disappeared when she looked into my eyes. I am sure that is their tactic to restrain us humans. I smiled again about the thought that I felt like a lab rat every time I go under with these beings.

"There's no way we can ever have a civilized one-on-one discussion. It is always diminishing in a way, an insult to my brilliant human mind, the top of the earthly animal kingdom," I thought. "Oh, well, maybe in another life."

I was awake and ready for anything. The being stared deeply inside my mind, knew my thoughts, and read my feelings. She analyzed me psychologically. I could sense she was measuring my feelings, ideas and worries. Yet, I tried my best to look and act calm. She knew that and stared. I was calm and very submissive, as I usually wanted to be and to act in this kind of situation, but my body would not cooperate unless I was injected with the laughing syrup. Inside my

216

brains and head, I had many questions. I knew I had to wait for my chance, just like she advised me.

"Be patient," she said.

Even if I wanted to say something, I was not allowed just yet and I had to obey.

Now the female being was talking to me. I did not ask her name because she was other than human, so I thought of her as an extraterrestrial if I were lucky. She did not address me by my name either, but I knew that she knew me, and she was more like a scientist. In other words, I thought she was someone more interested in observations of human behavior.

I was totally wrong.

The being assured me by saying, "You're my mission."

I was desperate. I wanted to know all, so she placed one of her hands on my temple and the other on the back of my head. I finally satisfied my curiosity. A few quick thoughts came through to me. I learned that she had always been there and had answered all my questions, so those feelings of trust weren't new to me after all. That's why they led me to trust her in a way. In truth, we had always been in communication. She was sort of a social worker to me and at the same time a psychologist in a way.

She became very real in her mesmerizing answers and didn't seem to hold anything back, and I felt very confident around her. I had a few questions of my own. I wanted to ask her if there was a God, what's the secret for immortality, or what do you think about us humans? But other questions came out instead. How did I get from point A to point B? Why doesn't my wife ever wake up when I'm being taken? Am I dreaming?

I was only confirming my fears with these questions. I really didn't feel the need to ask her profound questions about what people really wonder, and I knew why. Because, when I was at their telepathic level of understanding, I knew all the answers; they were there all my life in plain view.

I'm sure every human being has their own answers to many infinite questions. The truth is that we always seem to want to do what is wrong and bad; it is in our nature. We want to do our own thing and if anyone tries to help us out from going in the wrong direction, we go into auto destruct, get very upset, and become enemies with those who are trying to help us. We don't want anyone to interfere with our business. We can't handle interference with our ego.

The maximum wisdom of humans is the love we can spread among the least privileged, amongst our families and friends, as well as give respect to others, even the respect for lesser beings like animals.

The creature was very human, indeed; she was delicate in her manners and made me feel important. She acted exactly as we expect from a kind human soul.

I ran out of questions.

"We're going to take a tour," she finally said.

"A tour? Where?" I thought.

The being turned her head towards me and replied, "You'll see!"

She had a name, but I don't think I was bright enough to pick it up. I couldn't catch it, but it did sound something like "Farnsworth." So, I asked her if I could address her as "Mrs. Farnsworth," and she accepted with a smile.

"Great job!" I can swear she said.

I thought that it was a great maternal, loving name for her, even though she was an extraterrestrial being. I smiled back at her.

Mrs. Farnsworth showed me how to engage our minds using telepathy, which isn't that cool as humans may think, and I'll explain why. You wouldn't be able to hide anything from the other being; that included thoughts, doubts, feelings, remembrances, etc. Everything, literally everything, is all out in the open. Imagine that! Humans are all about secrets and privacy but not so with these beings; no wonder they are a bit more advanced than us insignificant human beings.

Walking around with Mrs. Farnsworth, I bumped into a heavyset, older woman. She was in her 60s and so frightened that I couldn't help but giggle a bit. She was under restraint, and all she could do was eyeball me and beg for help. I guess she thought I was a human like her. I transmitted positive thoughts to her mind, told her to be calm, and that everything was going to be over very soon.

Then, I looked the other way. My intentions were trying to be more tolerant and less emotional, so these beings could do their job and at the same time I could gather more information. I knew nothing was going to happen to this older woman anyway, and Mrs. Farnsworth assured me that the former wouldn't be able to remember a thing.

Mrs. Farnsworth explained that abductions take place as early as when the fetuses are formed in their mothers' womb, some as early as a month, all the way to the day of birth.

I remembered asking, "Why do you do that?"

It did bother me in a way. I felt that it was a traumatic experience.

She replied, "Humans are empty vessels. They need to be taught that was the way they were meant to be. You'll understand soon enough."

We stopped at a huge, solid, soft wall with a strange texture on it. It did open up like a movie screen with a super HD, crystal clear image. I could feel my pupils indirectly dilating in size when the giant screen the size of an IMAX Theater showed an incredible spectacular view of stars and galaxies, millions of them in deep space and in 3D. I tried to keep calm and be relaxed regardless of the fears I felt inside. I did not realize at that moment that we could probably be moving through space, although I never felt any kind of movement. I even thought that we were still at a parking lot down on Earth.

I guess I achieved some sort of equilibrium which helped me feel at ease and allowed a trust or special bonding with Mrs. Farnsworth. As we viewed this screen up close and personal, I gazed at the stars and nebulae at a range closer than watching it from Earth, I suppose.

I never had the opportunity to see through any telescopes, yet the universe was there in front of me. How lucky and blessed I felt at that moment. I always wanted to buy a telescope in the past and never did. If I had, I would have been disappointed looking up from Earth with so many obstacles in between, like the atmosphere, clouds, dust particles, rain, etc.

I finally had a chance to ask Mrs. Farnsworth more questions. I was on my own terms, and she allowed me to. I asked her how long they've been visiting us on Earth, and what was the purpose?

She simply replied very nicely that they had a mission like any other beings that exist out there in the universe. No one came down to Earth regarding us humans without a mission, too. Theirs was to take care of us, although they were just a tiny portion of the equation.

Our Earth is a garden. We are like the plants in this garden as well as everything that is and exists in our plane. All they do is follow instructions and that is to make sure we are being guided. This is because we quickly lose direction and vision.

I wondered if she meant humanity as a whole, or each single human.

I told her that we do not have a lot of choices: governments were already here, organizations, too. Society already tells you what it is that you need to do to fit in, or whatever you want to call it.

She kept gazing at the stars and made no comments.

Obviously, I held many thoughts since she knew my worries and human fears.

She looked away and said, "Just a few of you know the reality about your world, yet usually it's a truth humanity doesn't want to hear. It's still going to take some time, a very long time, for humans to reach the level of their true reality and the meaning of their place in the universe. First off, humans need to know where they stand in their own borrowed world."

Somehow, I was feeling embarrassed for all of humanity. I kind of knew what she meant, but it was impossible to force the world to use logic. It didn't make me feel any better. I felt like a low life being because part of the underdevelopment as humans in this universe was for us to feel superior and to have all the power so that we can be the only ones shining in this world.

A countless series of memories went through my head so real as if I had lived them through time and space. People talked in many languages I had never heard before. They were far more real than a real Hollywood movie. Most stories were splashed with blood, worthless wars, and despicable crimes against the essence of our immortal souls.

My shame was growing, and my heart couldn't help it.

She told me to calm down and avoid the vivid images.

I tried to forget all the cruelty of humans against their own kind.

I asked her, "Why do you bother checking on our health, skin, brains, mouths, skeletal structure, nose and ears, if your technology is far more advanced than ours? What's so important to you? Why do you even care?"

Mrs. Farnsworth simply replied that their job was to obey and that is exactly what they were doing.

I also had a vision in my head where I was shown a fish tank and was taking care of it constantly in order to keep all living things in there safe, healthy and clean. I wasn't too impressed with the answers, but maybe it was beyond my comprehension. Perhaps humans like to complicate things, and that is exactly where our issues begin.

I believe there is a God, and we are here because we chose to experience the awesome part of being a human in this world. Being human was loaned to us, and when our time comes, our spirit and soul go back to the Creator, and that's it.

"Why was I chosen?" I thought.

I realized I was not the only one who questioned the way I did. My point of view had to do with lineage. Regardless of how ordinary we may think we are, most of us aren't rich enough, smart enough or competent enough to stand there and question or demand answers from an ET who is here to do her job.

But her answer to my chosen question was, "Do not underestimate yourself."

She freaked me out, and I tried not to look amused.

Her deep thoughts continued. "Humans are a complex race of beings who value what is not important and label everything to make their lives more complicated. We enjoy sitting in the most important places amongst others who are just as equal and not less important. We think for some reason that our race is royalty and that the rest of the world is less privileged when in reality it is not, since we all are special to our Creator who treasures each one of us. When we learn that, then, and only then, will we be welcomed to the universe's biggest secrets and join the round table of our king. Lifespan is very important to humans even if they hate what their lives have become. Most can kill lesser beings or others just like them without any remorse. Humans also act without thinking and take many years to realize their mistakes because their pride is more important than accepting anything for their own good."

I reacted that I thought no one was going to come from a faraway place in the heavens to do a stupid psychological test.

Mrs. Farnsworth's Rhapsody

Mrs. Farnsworth countered, "We've been here since your very beginning, and our job is to record everything you do or wouldn't do."

"Well, I think that there is a purpose to whatever it is that you're doing, but I can't just believe this is a one-way street. What is it that you need to accomplish then?"

Her head, shaped like a supersized pear, moved every which way, slowly, and graciously, like a puppet moved by strings. Her slim hands and long fingers positioned themselves in a way that her body language inspired me to be more careful choosing my questions. She seemed so wise that I really needed to ask her something amazing. I thought in my head that I might never have the chance to be in this position ever again. I also learned that their goal is our goal and their accomplishment is likewise our accomplishment, so they teach us what we are and what we need to do. We are here to learn to be wise for the sake of our own humanity. It seems that we lack a great deal of it, and they're making sure we do just that. It takes time, patience, and since nothing can be forced on us, they can only hope we use our free will to choose right from wrong.

"We are here," she said, "to help those who want to be helped."

One thing was really the factor and key to my questions and that was when she said, "We are not your Redeemers."

My heart stopped on a dime. I knew it all along! Thank you, Jesus. I praised Him in my head.

A big wave of thoughts hit me, again. I doubted one more time that I was really there and that it wasn't a dream either.

"It's gotta be a dream. Oh, God, I want to wake up now."

Everything was so incredible, and the way it happened was so special to me than all the other times. This time was more clear and vivid. I learned history without the hidden mysteries of holding back the contaminated truth that can only come from human intervention. It's a damned truth that always serves our own ego and convenience like when we want to embellish or make someone a hero according to our perverse point of view. Also, it's often a certain truth with worthless theories, which are totally off the mark. Instead, I learned from Mrs. Farnsworth a worldly knowledge about this world circus we call Earth.

"Everything in our world on Earth was so wrong; how could that be?" I asked myself.

I was getting so depressed. I felt like I was in this world all these years living a darn lie, a worthless life, a total fraud.

Mrs. Farnsworth put one of her long, thin fingers on my forehead, and an explosion of thoughts and flashes of light were supered over the rest of what we call thoughts and emotions. And I was crying so hard that it was ridiculous. I couldn't stop it; it was a pitiful sight.

I kept saying, "We're so dark and so lost. We have no excuses."

My conclusion was that anything we do, if not in the purpose of helping our own kind, then the whole creation project was doomed. We've just wasted our time and our creator's.

We are so ignorant and despicable that we need to be reprogrammed. It doesn't matter what we do because soon we are lost and can't even see it. We lose our capacity to understand the real vision of things, our real intentions, and what motivated us to choose wrong over right.

Soon we become the judge of all things. If someone does not look like us, we pass this harsh judgment quickly and condemn their acts, and if someone doesn't think like us, we exterminate them. The worst part is when someone does wrong according to our society's moral standards. What we choose to do immediately is to crucify them without mercy.

How wrong is humanity!

We have a long way to go!

I was in a state of shock and weeping like a child who had lost his mother. My teeth were shivering because I realized how easy we could destroy our own selves. We have become worse than savages and have not learned self-control. I was desperate and feeling lost without direction about all these similar guilt trips.

Mrs. Farnsworth told me not to worry. She said that her intention was not to pass judgment on humanity, and that is why they were here. It was to help us to go through this learning process, and as soon as we learned, progress would come in due time. She made sure I knew that everything was okay and told me to keep my faith alive in my heart. They are doing their part, and we were called to do ours as well.

My time was up. I needed to go somewhere else. Many others were arriving.

"We have enough of you soldiers to fight your battles," she said.

I turned my head to her and wondered what she meant for a second, but I needed no answer. I knew exactly what the alien lady meant to say.

Soon, I settled into a pleasant and extended relaxation state and felt lifted into my bed back on Earth. I got up so quickly with a rested mind.

I said to myself, "Wow, what a weird dream!"

I really used this technique to deny my experiences. The only problem I had was that back in my bedroom and in the safety of my home, I saw Mrs. Farnsworth waving goodbye within a spotlight that went through the roof, soon darkened, and then she was gone. I was quite awake and could have denied it all I wanted but couldn't just pass it off as a dream any longer.

The very bright spotlight through the roof narrowed down and stayed there for a few seconds, enough that I saw it move like a flashlight. Then millions of particles the size of grains of salt began to fall down onto the carpet, and I placed my hands underneath the whole thing, but it disappeared instantly.

Afterword

I hope that my stories have enlightened you to the many mysteries and hidden dimensions. If you or someone you know are going through the same kind of experiences, rest assured that you are not alone. There are countless humans like me who have been given this gift for unknown reasons. I can only speculate that we have a certain energy signature that resonates with paranormal and extraterrestrial beings such that they seek us out as witnesses, messengers and even teachers for the spiritual events that unfold before us. Just how we are to be witnesses, messengers and teachers remains a mystery and may not occur entirely in this lifetime.

I can only say that if I have opened your eyes to the truth of what I have experienced and if it helps you out to understand otherworldly experiences, then I guess I have fulfilled the messenger and teacher part of my calling: to pass clarity and understanding to my fellow human beings. As to the witnessing part, I've been told by many entities within the dimensions that this part of my calling will come when my soul passes from this plane.

Thank you for your understanding, and I wish all of you the best. I plan to write a second volume of "Into the Dimensions" in the near future and share with you more incredible, but true, paranormal and extraterrestrial encounters in my life.

Biography

Carlo S. Carnevalini was born in Managua, Nicaragua in 1962. At 5 years old he had ,his first extraterrestrial experience with Short Greys on his grandparents' farm called Los Chaguites. His paranormal and extraterrestrial encounters continued throughout his youth and into his teen years with most of his family and friends belittling or debunking him for such strange stories.

After a civil war broke out in Nicaragua, Carlo escaped to Los Angeles, California in 1979, but his experiences followed him there. He had both dark visions of demons and devils as well as epiphanies of angels and the divine creator, both of which deeply affected his devout Catholic upbringing. Carlo married and moved to Miami Florida, but his disturbing experiences continued with visits to motherships, etheric dimensions and unknown planets. Often ET beings would give him cautionary messages to bring back to Earth that mankind is too violent and must change its ways. By his own desire to not drive his beloved wife crazy with his continuous experiences, he ended by mutual consent a fourteen-year marriage.

Today he lives a quiet life outside LA writing his memoirs and books about his lifelong exposure to the unexplained paranormal and extraterrestrial dimensions.

Parting Words

We are all
infinite, indestructible, spiritual souls
having a temporary physical incarnation
on this planet.

Made in the USA
Middletown, DE
16 July 2022

69524257R00146